UPGRADING TO
by Charlie Russel an

ISBN:0-7821-2190-X; 448 pag

The *original* Windows upgrade book helps over 100 million Windows users painlessly switch to Windows 98.

EXPERT GUIDE TO WINDOWS 98
by Mark Minasi, Eric Christiansen, and Kristina Shapar

ISBN:0-7821-1974-3; 944 pages; $49.99; 1CD

Contains over 1,000 pages of the most advanced (often undocumented) Windows 98 secrets from Mark Minasi, the country's #1 Windows authority. The CD includes an electronic version of the book, valuable utilities, and screen-cam instructions by the author himself!

WINDOWS® 98 QUICK REFERENCE

SYBEX INC.

San Francisco • Paris • Düsseldorf • Soest

Associate Publisher: Gary Masters

Contracts and Licensing Manager: Kristine Plachy

Compiler and Editor: Pat Coleman

Acquisitions & Developmental Editor: Maureen Adams

Project Editor: Shelby Zimmerman

Book Designer: Maureen Forys, Happenstance Type-O-Rama

Desktop Publisher: Maureen Forys, Happenstance Type-O-Rama

Production Coordinator: Rebecca Rider

Cover Designer: Design Site

Cover Illustrator: Design Site

The contents of this book have been adapted from Peter Dyson's *Windows 98 Instant Reference*.

Screen reproductions produced with Collage Complete. Collage Complete is a trademark of Inner Media Inc.

SYBEX is a registered trademark of SYBEX Inc.

TRADEMARKS: SYBEX has attempted throughout this book to distinguish proprietary trademarks from descriptive terms by following the capitalization style used by the manufacturer.

The author and publisher have made their best efforts to prepare this book, and the content is based upon final release software whenever possible. Portions of the manuscript may be based upon pre-release versions supplied by software manufacturer(s). The author and the publisher make no representation or warranties of any kind with regard to the completeness or accuracy of the contents herein and accept no liability of any kind including but not limited to performance, merchantability, fitness for any particular purpose, or any losses or damages of any kind caused or alleged to be caused directly or indirectly from this book.

Library of Congress Card Number: 98-84537

ISBN: 0-7821-2286-8

Manufactured in the United States of America

10 9 8 7 6 5 4 3 2 1

TABLE OF CONTENTS

INTRODUCTION

introduction

Windows 98 represents the next evolutionary step in the progression of Windows operating systems. It is bigger, faster, slicker, and more capable than anything that has gone before. Windows 98 supports more kinds of hardware and includes much more application software than any previous version of Windows.

Not only does Windows 98 include the wildly popular Internet Explorer Web browser, but it also includes several other important Web-based tools for conferencing, e-mail, Web page creation, and Web publishing. You also get a complete set of capable but easy-to-use system tools for tasks such as defragmenting disks, compressing files, testing disks, and monitoring your system. Windows 98 has more online help information than ever before and includes a whole flock of Wizards to guide you through some of the more complex configuration options. Also new in Windows 98 are the Troubleshooters, which you can use to track down and isolate complex system configuration and hardware problems.

The Classic Windows Interface

When you first install Windows 98, you will see the classic Windows user interface. It is similar to the interface in earlier versions of Windows: A single click selects an object or an icon, a double click opens the object or starts the application, and a right click opens a pop-up menu you can use to work with the selected object.

As an example, this is what the Control Panel looks like when you use classic Windows:

The Active Desktop Interface

If you are comfortable using the Internet, the Web, and the Internet Explorer Web browser, you can choose to use the Active Desktop instead of classic Windows. In this case, everything works just like it does on a Web page.

All the familiar Windows Desktop icons appear with their names underlined, and when you place the mouse cursor on them, the cursor changes to a hand to indicate a link. And you no longer double-click. Simply place the cursor on an icon or an object to select it, click to open it or run the application, and (just as with classic Windows), right-click to open the pop-up menu. As an example, this is what the Windows Control Panel looks like using the Active Desktop:

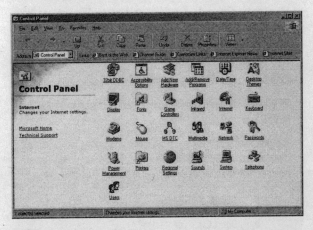

With the Active Desktop, you get a consistent browserlike view of everything—from the files on your local hard disk to your corporate intranet to the Internet itself. Neither interface is better than the other; they are just different. And the choice is yours:

- ▶ You can use classic Windows.

- ▶ You can use the Active Desktop.

- ▶ Or you can switch between them as you see fit.

This book uses the Windows Active Desktop, and the descriptions of how things work reflect this.

What Else Is New in Windows 98

In addition to the Active Desktop, there's lots more new stuff in Windows 98. Here are some of the highlights:

Support for Multiple Displays   Lets you use more than two monitors at the same time.

Drive Converter (FAT32)   Allows you to convert from the older 16-bit FAT file system to a newer, more efficient system.

Maintenance Wizard   Runs Disk Defragmenter, ScanDisk, and Disk Cleanup so that you get the most out of your hard disk system. If you have a DriveSpace 3 volume on your system, the Maintenance Wizard will also run Compression Agent.

Task Scheduler   Provides a way to schedule routine applications.

TV Viewer   Brings conventional television broadcast reception to a PC near you.

Troubleshooters   Let you track down and isolate hardware and configuration-related problems from inside the Windows Help system. Troubleshooters are available for:

- Dial-Up Networking
- Direct Cable Connection
- Display
- DriveSpace
- Hardware Conflicts
- Memory
- Modem
- MS-DOS Programs

▶ Networking

▶ PC Card

▶ Print

▶ Sound

▶ Startup and Shutdown

▶ The Microsoft Network

Connection Wizard   Helps you select or configure a connection to your Internet service provider.

Outlook Express   Creates, receives, and manages your e-mail.

NetMeeting   Provides audio and video conferencing features and an online whiteboard.

FrontPage Express   Helps you create Web pages in HTML.

Personal Web Server   Supports your own local Web server.

Web Publishing Wizard   Loads your Web pages onto the Web server.

Internet Explorer   Brings the latest in Web browsers to Windows 98.

How This Book Is Organized

This book presents the most common Windows 98 features, applications, and configuration options listed in alphabetic order. Most of the entries start with the Windows icon or menu selection you actually use to access the specific feature under discussion. Application toolbars and menu selections are discussed in detail, and configuration options are described in numbered steps for ease of use. If a feature is known by a name other than its official name, you'll find a →*See* cross-reference from that name to its official name.

Conventions Used in This Book

This book uses just a couple of special typographical conventions. Anything that you have to type, such as a command name or a program name, is in **boldface**. Web addresses, also known as URLs, are in a `monospace` font.

introduction

Additional information appears throughout the book in the form of Notes, Tips, and Warnings:

✔ n o t e

Notes provide additional information about a specific topic.

▲ t i p

Tips give you clues on how to make better use of a Windows feature or detail shortcut methods you can use to get the same result.

✖ w a r n i n g

Warnings alert you to the potential dangers of using (or abusing) certain features.

WINDOWS 98 QUICK REFERNCE

Active Desktop

In Windows 98, you can use a conventional Windows interface similar to that in earlier versions of Windows, or you can use the Active Desktop. The Active Desktop brings the world of the Web right to the Windows 98 Desktop, allowing you to replace the static Windows wallpaper with a fully configurable, full-screen Web page. The Active Desktop can contain other Web pages, dynamic HTML, and even Java components such as stock tickers and ActiveX controls, and you can add these elements to the Taskbar or to a folder.

✔ **n o t e**

You can combine the Active Desktop and Internet Explorer's subscription capabilities to create your own personal push-content client, displaying data on your Desktop from whatever sources interest you. For example, you can display a continuously updating stock ticker or sports results right on your Desktop, assuming of course that you have continuous Internet access.

To set up your Active Desktop, choose Start ➤ Settings ➤ Active Desktop, and you will see three options: View As Web Page, Customize My Desktop, and Update Now. You can also right-click the Desktop and select Active Desktop from the menu.

View As Web Page

Turns on the Active Desktop interface. Selecting this option a second time removes the checkmark and turns the Active Desktop off again.

Customize My Desktop

Opens the Display Properties dialog box. You can also right-click the Desktop and select Properties, or if you prefer, choose Start ➤ Settings ➤ Control Panel and select the Display icon. The Display Properties dialog box contains six tabs, but here we are only concerned with the following two:

Background   Lets you choose an HTML document or a picture to use as your Desktop background. In the Wallpaper box, select the background you want to use, or click Pattern to choose or modify the background pattern. You can also click the Browse button to locate a file or to go directly to a Web site to find the HTML document you are interested in using as a background. To cover your entire Desktop with a small wallpaper image, select Tile from the Display box, or choose Center if you prefer to see the image centered. Click the Apply button to see the effect of your changes before you exit the Display Properties dialog box, or click OK to accept the changes and close the dialog box.

▲ t i p

You can also right-click any Web page graphic that takes your fancy and then click Set As Wallpaper.

Web   Lets you select and organize Active Desktop elements. At the top of the tab, you will see a representation of your Desktop, indicating the location of any Active Desktop elements. These same elements are listed in the box below. To add a new element such as a stock ticker or a weather map, click New to open the New Active Desktop Item dialog box. If you want to browse through Microsoft's Active Desktop Gallery on Microsoft's Web site for a component to add, click Yes. To select a different Web site, click No, and then enter the address or URL for the Web site, or click the Browse button to locate it. Be sure that the *View my Active Desktop as a Web page* box is checked if you want your Desktop to look like a Web page.

✔ n o t e

You can also right-click any link on a Web page, drag it to your Desktop, and then click Create Active Desktop Item Here.

Update Now

Updates the Desktop contents right now to display any changes you have made.

▲ t i p

Sometimes the Active Desktop can get hidden behind application windows while you are working on a project. If this happens, click the Show Desktop button on the Taskbar to redisplay the Desktop. The Show Desktop button also appears in many other places in Windows, including the Browse dialog box.

Add New Hardware

 Guides you through the process of adding new hardware to your system using the New Hardware Wizard. This Wizard automatically makes the appropriate changes to the Registry and to the configuration files so that Windows 98 can recognize and support your new hardware. Be sure you have installed or connected your new hardware before you go any further.

To install a Plug and Play device on your system, follow these steps:

1. Turn off your computer.

2. Connect or install the new device according to the manufacturer's instructions.

3. Turn your computer back on again to restart Windows 98. Windows will locate your new hardware automatically and install the appropriate software for you.

If Windows 98 does not find your new Plug and Play device, check that it is installed properly, and if you can, confirm that the device actually works and is not defective in some way.

If the device you want to install is not a Plug and Play device, follow these steps instead:

1. Turn off your computer.

2. Connect or install the new device according to the manufacturer's instructions.

3. Turn your computer back on again to restart Windows 98.

4. Choose Start ➤ Settings ➤ Control Panel, and then click the Add New Hardware icon to open the Add New Hardware Wizard. Click the Next button.

You must next decide whether you want Windows 98 to automatically detect your hardware or if you want to identify the hardware yourself.

5. Choose Yes if you want Windows 98 to search for your new hardware. You will be warned that Windows may spend several minutes searching and that your machine could quit functioning during the search. Click Next.

A status monitor indicates the progress of the search. Depending on the amount and type of hardware, the detection process could take several minutes.

6. If you don't want Windows 98 to try to detect the device, click No, and then click Next. A dialog box will prompt you to select the new device from a list. Click the hardware type you are installing, and then click Next.

7. From this point on, the dialog boxes depend on the type of hardware you are installing; simply follow the instructions on the screen to complete the installation.

Add/Remove Programs

Installs or uninstalls individual elements of the Windows 98 operating system itself or certain application programs. Installing or removing application or system software components in this way enables Windows 98 to modify all the appropriate system and configuration files automatically so that the information in them stays current and correct.

To start Add/Remove Programs, choose Start ➤ Settings ➤ Control Panel, and then click the Add/Remove Programs icon to open the Add/Remove Programs Properties dialog box. This dialog box contains four tabs if you are connected to a local area network; otherwise, it contains three tabs.

Install/Uninstall Tab

To install a new program using the Add/Remove Programs applet, follow these steps:

1. Select the Install/Uninstall tab if it isn't already selected, and then click the Install button.

5

2. Put the application program CD or floppy disk in the appropriate drive, and click the Next button to display a setup or install message, describing the program to be installed.

3. To continue with the installation process, click the Finish button. To make any changes, click Back and repeat the procedure.

To uninstall a program previously installed under Windows 98, you must follow a different process. The list of programs that have uninstall capability (not all of them do) will appear in the display box of the Install/Uninstall tab. Click the program you want to uninstall, and then click the Add/Remove button. You may see a warning message about removing the application. You will be told when the uninstall is finished.

✔ n o t e

Once you remove an application using Add/Remove Programs, you will have to reinstall it from the original program disks or CD if you change your mind and decide you want to use it again. You can't just copy the files from the Recycle Bin back into their original folders because settings from the Start button and perhaps from the Windows Registry may have been deleted.

Windows Setup Tab

Some components of the Windows 98 operating system are optional, and you can install or uninstall them as you wish; the Windows Clipboard Viewer is an example. Select the Windows Setup tab to display a list of such components with checkboxes on the left. If the box has a checkmark in it, the component is currently installed. If the checkbox is gray, only some elements of that component are installed; to see what is included in a component, click the Details button. Follow these steps to add a Windows 98 component:

1. Click the appropriate checkbox.

2. If the component consists of several elements, click the Details button to display a list of them, and check the boxes you want to install.

3. Click OK to display the Windows Setup tab.

4. Click the Apply button, and then click OK.

To remove a Windows 98 component from your system, follow these steps:

1. Click the Details button to see a complete list of the individual elements in the component you want to uninstall.

2. Clear the checkmark from the checkboxes of the elements you want to uninstall, and then click OK to open the Windows Setup tab.

3. Click the Apply button, and then click OK.

Startup Disk Tab

A startup disk is a floppy disk with which you can start, or "boot," your computer if something happens to your hard drive. When you originally installed Windows 98, you were asked if you wanted to create a startup disk. If you didn't do it at that time or if the disk you created then is not usable, you can create one now. Simply insert a disk with at least 1.2MB capacity in the appropriate drive, click Create Disk, and follow the instructions on the screen.

Network Install Tab

In some cases, you can also install a program directly from a network using the Network Install tab. If the Network Install tab is not present in the Add/Remove Programs Properties dialog box, this feature may not have been enabled on your computer or on your network; see your system administrator for more details.

If the Install/Uninstall tab is selected, your system is currently connected to the network, and you can click Install followed by Next to find the setup program for your network.

If the Network Install tab is selected, follow the instructions on the screen.

Address Book

Manages your e-mail addresses, as well as your voice, fax, modem, and cellular phone numbers. Once you enter an e-mail address in your Address Book, you can select it from a list rather than type it in every time. To open the Address Book, choose Start ➤ Programs ➤ Internet Explorer ➤ Address Book, or click the Address Book icon on the Outlook Express toolbar.

Importing an Existing Address Book

Address Book can import information from an existing address book in any of the following formats:

- ▶ Windows Address Book

- ▶ Microsoft Exchange Personal Address Book

- ▶ Microsoft Internet Mail for Windows 3.1 Address Book

- ▶ Netscape Address Book

- ▶ Netscape Communicator Address Book

- ▶ Eudora Pro or Lite Address Book

- ▶ Lightweight Directory Access Protocol (LDAP)

- ▶ Comma-separated text file

To import information from one of these address books, follow these steps:

1. Choose Start ➤ Programs ➤ Internet Explorer ➤ Address Book, or click the Address Book icon on the Outlook Express toolbar.

2. Choose File ➤ Import ➤ Address Book to open the Address Book Import Tool dialog box.

3. Select the file you want to import, and click Import.

Address Book Window

The main Address Book window lists the names and e-mail addresses of individuals and groups of individuals, along with business and home phone information if it is available.

The Address Book toolbar contains the following buttons:

 New Contact   Opens the Properties dialog box.

 New Group   Opens the Group Properties dialog box.

 Properties   Displays the Properties dialog box for the selected entry.

Delete Removes the selected entry.

 Find Opens the Find People dialog box so that you can look up people and businesses using the Internet.

 Print Prints the address list.

 Send Mail Opens Outlook Express so that you can send e-mail.

Some of these functions are repeated on the Address Book menus, particularly the File, Edit, and Tools menus. The View menu contains options that you can use to configure the toolbar, icons, and entry sort order.

Creating a New Address Book Entry

To add a new entry to your Address Book, click the New Contact button on the Address Book toolbar or choose File ➤ New Contact to open the Properties dialog box. This dialog box has six tabs:

Personal Lets you enter personal information including the person's first, middle, and last names, a nickname, and an e-mail address. If the person has more than one e-mail address, click Add and continue entering addresses.

Home Allows you to enter additional information about this contact; enter as much or as little information as makes sense here.

Business Allows you to enter business-related information; again, enter as much or as little information as makes sense.

Other Offers a chance to store additional information about this contact as a set of text notes.

NetMeeting Lets you enter NetMeeting information such as a person's conferencing e-mail address and server name. If NetMeeting is not installed on your system, this tab will be called Conferencing.

Digital IDs Allows you to specify a digital certificate for use with an e-mail address.

Setting Up a New Group

You can create groups of e-mail addresses to make it easy to send a message to all the members of the group. You can group people any way you like—by job title, musical taste, or sports team allegiance. When you want to send e-mail to everyone in the group, simply use the group name instead of selecting each e-mail address individually. To create a new group, follow these steps:

1. Click the New Group icon on the Address Book toolbar or choose File ➤ New Group to open the Group Properties dialog box.

2. In the Group Name field, enter the name you want to use for this group.

3. If you want to add a person to this new group who is not yet in your Address Book, click New Contact to open the Properties dialog box. Enter the information, and click OK.

4. Click Select Members to open the Select Members dialog box. Add the names of those people who already have entries in your Address Book into this new group. Click OK when you are done to return to the Properties dialog box.

5. Use the Notes field for comments about the group. You might note that they meet at the local bookstore on Thursday evenings at 7:30, for example.

6. When you have finished adding members to the group, click OK.

You will now see the name of this new group displayed in the Address Book main window. To send e-mail to all the group members, select the group name, and click the Send Mail button on the toolbar.

Address Toolbar

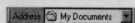 Shows the location of the page currently being displayed in the main window; this may be a URL on the Internet or on an intranet or a file or folder stored on your hard disk.

To go to another page, click the arrow at the right end of the Address toolbar to select the appropriate entry, or simply type a new location. When you start to type an address that you have previously entered, the AutoComplete feature recognizes the address and completes the entry for you.

The Address toolbar is available in most Windows 98 applications, including the Explorer, Internet Explorer, My Computer, the Control Panel, and others.

Backup

Creates an archive copy of one or more files and folders on your hard disk and then restores them to your hard disk in the event of a disk or controller failure or some other unforeseen event. Everybody's heard about making backups, but why should you make a backup?

To protect against hard disk failure. A hard disk can fail at almost any time, but when it does, it is always at the most inconvenient moment.

To protect against accidental deletion of a file. If you work on many projects, your chances of accidentally deleting a file are far greater than if you work on only one at a time.

To create an archive at the end of a project. You can make a backup that contains all the files relating to a single project when the work is done; then if you need to refer to the files again, you know where to find them.

These are the main reasons to make a backup, but there are others. You might back up the files of a terminating employee in case the computer is reassigned within your department or is transferred to another department. In either case, the new user will likely clean up the hard disk—in other words, delete all the most important files. In addition, making a backup is one way to transfer a large number of files from one computer system to another. Finally, you should always back up before making a substantial change to your system, such as installing new hardware, upgrading the operating system, or making a major configuration change to your application software.

Once you decide to make a backup, you need to plan your backup strategy—and most important—stick to it. With no plan, you will simply accumulate floppy disks or tapes haphazardly, you will waste tapes, and you will waste time looking for a file when you need to restore a file deleted by accident.

So how often should you make a backup? For an answer that fits the way you work, consider these questions:

▶ How often do your data files change? Every day? Every week? Every month?

▶ How important to your day-to-day operations are these files? Can you work without them? How long would it take you to re-create them?

▶ How much will it cost to replace lost files in terms of time spent and business lost?

In our computerized world, it takes hours to create an HTML page with just the right look or a budget spreadsheet that everyone agrees to, but either can be lost or destroyed in milliseconds. A hard-disk failure, a mistaken delete command, overwriting the file with an earlier version with the same name— these can destroy a file just as surely as fire, flood, or earthquake. You just have to lose one important file to become an instant convert for life to a program of regular, planned backups.

To start the Windows 98 backup program, choose Start ➤ Programs ➤ Accessories ➤ System Tools ➤ Backup. The first time you start the program, a dialog box welcomes you to Microsoft Backup and leads directly into the Backup Wizard.

Using the Backup Wizard

Using the Backup Wizard is a quick and easy way to learn about backups; it gets you going quickly with the minimum of technical knowledge. Check Create a New Backup Job, and then click OK in this opening dialog box to start the Wizard. If you would rather not use the Wizard, click Close; you can always restart it from the toolbar inside the Backup program if you change your mind.

The Wizard walks you through the following sequence of dialog boxes. Click the Next button when you have made your choice to advance to the next dialog box; click Back to retrace your steps, and click Cancel if you change your mind about using the Wizard.

What to Back Up You can back up all files and folders on your computer or selected files and folders; you can also back up only those files that have changed since the last time you made a backup.

Where to Back Up   Select a destination drive for the backup. You can back up to a network drive, but check with your system administrator before you do so for the first time.

How to Back Up   You can compare the backup against the original copies of your files to ensure that the files are backed up properly, and you can specify whether Backup should compress your files as they are backed up to save space on the destination drive.

Name the Backup Job   Finally, you have to give this whole set of backup configuration information a name. This allows you to use this configuration, also known as a backup job, in the future simply by referring to the name.

Click the Start button to begin the backup; a small progress indicator tracks the backup as it proceeds.

A time will come when you want a little more control over your backups, and that is when you stop using the Wizard and take charge of the process yourself. At the Welcome dialog box, rather than invoking the Wizard, click Cancel to go right into the Backup program.

Backup Window

The Backup program provides the following toolbar buttons to help automate the backup process:

 New Backup Job   Defines a new backup job from scratch.

 Open Backup Job   Reuses a previously saved backup configuration.

 Save Job   Saves the backup job currently in use.

 Select Items   Helps you choose the items to back up.

 Deselect Items   Helps to exclude items from the backup.

 Backup Wizard   Starts the Backup Wizard running within the Backup program.

 Restore Wizard   Starts the Restore Wizard running within the Backup program.

Bb backup

 Job Options Lets you look at or change the job configuration information.

 List Displays information using the List view.

 Details Displays information in the Details view.

 Help Gives you access to the Help system.

✔ n o t e

Many toolbar buttons give access to the same functions as the drop-down menus.

Using the Backup program involves essentially the same tasks that the Backup Wizard does for you—selecting the files, deciding where to put them, and specifying how the backup should actually be made.

What to Back Up

If you have previously specified and saved a backup job, you can select it for use again from the list in the Backup Job box. That done, all you have to do is click the Start button to begin the backup.

If you don't have a previously saved backup job or if you want to do things a little differently this time, the first task is to decide which files to back up. You can back up all the files and folders selected in the Backup window, or you can back up only files that have changed along with any new files never before backed up.

In the Backup window, check the box next to the files and folders you want to back up. A blue checkmark indicates that the folder or file is selected for backup; a gray checkmark indicates that some of the files in the folder or on the drive have been selected for backup.

Where to Back Up

The next task is to select the destination device or drive for the backup and to name the backup file itself. To check the number of files you have selected for this backup and to see the total number of bytes, choose View ➤ Selected

Information. In this way, you can verify that the files you chose will actually fit on the destination device.

How to Back Up

The last part of the process is to review the backup configuration settings. Choose Job ➤ Options, click the Options button at the bottom of the Backup window, or click the Job Options button on the toolbar to open the Backup Job Options dialog box.

Across the top of the Backup Job Options dialog box are the following tabs:

General   Lets you specify that the backed-up data are compared against the original files to ensure the data were properly backed up. You can also specify how data compression is performed and how you want the Backup program to respond if it finds that the medium (tape, disk, or CD) you are using already contains a backup.

Password   Lets you protect a backup with a password that can be a maximum of eight characters. Passwords are case-sensitive, so StarTrek is not the same as startrek. You will need to remember this password because you will not be able to restore the files contained in this backup without it.

Type   Lets you choose how the backup is made. You can back up all the files you selected, or you can specify one of the following:

>**Differential Backup**   Backs up all the selected files that changed since the last All Selected Files backup. When the backup is complete, the archive bit for each file is left on.

>**Incremental Backup**   Backs up all the selected files that have changed since the last Incremental or All Selected Files backup. When the backup is complete, the archive bit for each file is turned off.

Exclude   Lets you specify file types that you want to exclude from this backup; use the Add and Remove buttons to select files for exclusion.

Report   Lets you specify the elements you want to include in the backup report. You can also specify that the backup is performed as an unattended backup without message boxes or prompts.

Advanced Lets you specify that the Windows Registry information is always included in the backup; otherwise, the Registry is only backed up when you include the Windows folder. This is always a good idea, so be sure to check this box.

All that remains is to click the Start button to begin the backup.

Setting Preferences

Choose Tools ➤ Preferences to open the Preferences dialog box, which is used to specify three general Backup options.

Check the first box to turn off the opening Welcome dialog box displayed when Backup is first started. Check the second box to ensure that the Windows Registry is always backed up if the Windows directory is included in the backup, and check the third box to display the number and size of the files that constitute the backup.

Once you are satisfied that everything is as it should be, choose Job ➤ Save or Job ➤ Save As to save all the configuration details of this backup as a separate backup job. You can also click the Save Job button on the toolbar for this same purpose.

Browse

Browse The Browse button is available in many common dialog boxes when you have to choose or enter a file name, find a folder, or specify a Web address or URL. Clicking the Browse button or the Find File button opens the Browse dialog box.

You can look through folders on any disk on any shared computer on the network to find the file you want. When you find the file, folder, computer, or Web site, double-click it to open, import, or enter it in a text box.

CD Player

Allows you to play audio compact discs on your CD-ROM drive. Choose Start ➤ Programs ➤ Accessories ➤ Entertainment ➤ CD Player to open the CD Player dialog box.

CD Player Dialog Box

The toolbar immediately beneath the menu bar contains the options described below. If you don't see these buttons when you open the CD Player, choose View ➤ Toolbar.

Edit Play List   Creates a list defining which tracks of one or more CDs will be played. Use this list to play the tracks you like and avoid those you don't.

Track Time Elapsed   Displays the elapsed time in the CD Player dialog box.

Track Time Remaining   Displays the time remaining in the CD Player dialog box.

Disc Time Remaining   Displays the remaining time the disc has to play.

Random Track Order   Plays the CD tracks in a random order. Normally, the tracks play in sequential order, starting with the first track. If you have a multidisc CD-ROM drive, you can use this option to play tracks from each CD in random order.

Continuous Play   Plays the CD continuously. Normally, it stops when the last track finishes playing.

Intro Play   Plays the first segments of tracks. You can use this option to search for specific tracks or pieces.

The CD Player dialog box has three menus that you can use to access the toolbar functions.

Disc Menu

Allows you to exit the CD Player dialog box or to build a play list from the available tracks on the identified CD. Choose Disc ➤ Edit Play List to open the Disc Settings dialog box. Select a track from Available Tracks, and then click Add to add a track to the Play List or click Remove to delete a track. Clear All clears all tracks from the Play List, and Reset restores the Play List to match the Available List. With the Set Name option, you can identify the tracks with an easy-to-remember title.

View Menu

Allows you to display the Toolbar, Disc/Track Info (which identifies the CD name, title, and track currently playing), and the Status bar at the bottom of the dialog box. From the View menu, you can choose to display the Track Time Elapsed, Track Time Remaining, or Disc Time Remaining. You can also set the Volume Control.

Options Menu

Allows you to play the CD in Random Order, Continuous Play, or Intro Play. Choose Options ➤ Preferences to open the Preferences dialog box and set the following:

Stop CD Playing on Exit   Stops the playing of the current CD when the CD Player is closed.

Save Settings on Exit   Saves the CD settings when the CD Player is closed.

Show Tool Tips   Displays the pop-up description of the toolbar buttons when you place the pointer over them.

Intro Play Length (seconds)   Specifies the playing time of the intro.

Display Font   Determines whether the track or disc time remaining or elapsed displays in a large or small font.

Playing the CD

You can control the CD by clicking the following buttons:

 Play   Starts the CD.

 Pause   Stops the CD until you press Play.

 Stop   Interrupts the playing of the CD.

 Previous Track   Replays the previous track.

 Skip Backwards   Moves backward through the current track bit by bit.

 Skip Forwards   Moves forward through the current track bit by bit.

Next Track Plays the next track.

 Eject Ejects the CD.

Channels

→See *Internet Explorer*

Chat

→See *NetMeeting*

Clipboard

A temporary storage place for data. You can use the Cut and Copy commands as well as the Windows screen capture commands to place data on the Clipboard. The Paste command then copies the data from the Clipboard to a receiving document, perhaps in another application. You cannot edit the Clipboard contents; however, you can view and save the information stored in the Clipboard by using the Clipboard Viewer, or you can paste the contents of the Clipboard into Notepad.

✖ w a r n i n g

The Clipboard only holds one piece of information at a time, so cutting or copying onto the Clipboard overwrites any existing contents.

Closing Windows

Closing an application program window terminates the operations of that program. In Windows 98, you can close windows in a number of ways:

▶ Click the Close button in the upper-right corner of the program title bar.

▶ Choose Control ➤ Close (identified by the icon to the left of the program name in the title bar) or simply double-click the Control Menu icon.

- Choose File ➤ Close or File ➤ Exit within the application.

- If the application is minimized on the Taskbar, right-click the application's icon and choose Close or press Alt+F4.

Connection Wizard

Walks you through the steps of setting up your Internet connection. All you need is an account with an ISP (Internet service provider), and you're all set. You can start the Connection Wizard in several ways:

- Click the Connect to the Internet icon on the Desktop.

- Choose Start ➤ Programs ➤ Internet Explorer ➤ Connection Wizard.

- From the Windows 98 Help system, choose Using the Internet Connection Wizard topic.

- Choose Start ➤ Settings ➤ Control Panel ➤ Internet to open the Internet Properties dialog box, and then select the Connection tab and click the Connect button.

- In Internet Explorer, choose View ➤ Internet Options to open the Internet Options dialog box, and then select the Connection tab and click the Connect button.

No matter which method you use, you first see the Welcome screen; click the Next button to continue. The Setup Options dialog box gives you three choices:

- Open a new account with an ISP. Select the first option if you do not have an account. The Wizard takes you through the steps of finding an ISP and starting an account and sets up the dial-up link for you.

- Establish a connection to an existing Internet account. Select the second option to set up a connection to your existing Internet account or to revise the settings for your current account.

- Make no change to your existing account. If you choose this option and click the Next button, the Wizard closes because there is nothing for it to do.

Creating a New Connection to the Internet

To create a new dial-up connection to the Internet, start the Connection Wizard, and then follow these steps:

1. In the opening dialog box, choose the first option to select an ISP and set up a new Internet account, and then click Next.

2. The Connection Wizard now begins the automatic part of the setup by loading programs from your original Windows 98 CD. You may be asked to restart your computer; the Wizard will resume automatically. Be sure you complete all the steps; otherwise, the Wizard may not be able to set up your connection properly.

3. If you have a modem, the Wizard attempts to locate an ISP in your area and sets up the appropriate Dial-Up Networking software on your system. Follow the prompts on the screen to complete the setup.

Modifying an Existing Connection to the Internet

You can modify your existing Internet account settings at any time. Start the Connection Wizard, and follow these steps:

1. In the opening dialog box, select the second option to set up a new connection to an existing Internet account.

2. Choose the method you use to connect to the Internet, either by phone line or through your local area network, and click Next.

3. In the Dial-Up Connection dialog box, check the Use an Existing Dial-Up Connection box, select the connection from the list box, and click the Next button.

4. You'll then be asked if you want to modify the settings for this connection. Click Yes, and then click Next to open the Phone Number dialog box where you can enter the phone number to dial to make the connection.

5. In the next dialog box, enter your user name and password information, and click Next.

6. In the Advanced Settings dialog box you are asked if you want to change any of the advanced settings for this connection, such as connection type, logon script file name, and IP address. You should only change these settings when your ISP or system administrator tells you to and provides the new information to use. Click Next.

7. You'll then be asked if you want to set up an Internet e-mail account; click Yes and then Next to specify whether you want to use an existing account or create a new one. If you opt to continue using an existing account, you will be asked to confirm your e-mail account settings; if you establish a new account, you will have to enter this information from scratch. Click Next.

8. Next, you'll be asked if you want to set up an Internet news account; follow the instructions on the screen.

9. Finally, click the Finish button to complete the configuration and close the Wizard.

Connect to the Internet

→See Connection Wizard

Control Panel

Provides a way to establish settings and defaults for all sorts of important Windows features. To access the Control Panel, choose Start ➤ Settings ➤ Control Panel.

If you are using the conventional Windows interface, you will see a window that looks like this:

22

To open an applet, double-click it, or click once on its icon to select it and then choose File ➤ Open.

If you are using the Active Desktop and you have View As Web Page turned on, you will see a much different Control Panel:

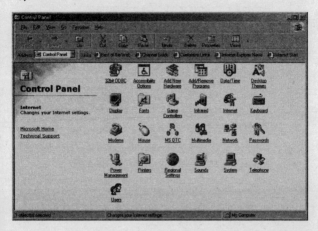

The Control Panel now looks and works like a Web page displayed in a browser. All the names of the applets are underlined, and the mouse pointer turns into a hand when you move the cursor over an icon. You will also see a short description of what each Control Panel applet does on the left side of the window. More important, it now takes only a single mouse-click to open an applet.

The Control Panel window is similar to all folder windows, and you can modify it through the View menu. In View As Web Page mode, you can also click the View button on the toolbar to cycle through four views of the Control Panel contents. Click the arrow next to the View button to open another version of the View menu.

Copying Floppy Disks

To copy a floppy disk, use the Copy Disk command. The disks used must be of the same type—for example, a 3½" high-density disk must be copied to another 3½" high-density disk. Any information on the receiving disk is replaced with the data from the source disk. Follow these steps:

1. Open Explorer and find the floppy disk drives you want to copy to and from.

▲ t i p

You can copy to and from the same drive. You will be prompted when to change
from the source to the destination disk.

2. Right-click the drive to open the pop-up menu.

3. Choose Copy Disk to open the Copy Disk dialog box.

4. On the left, select the disk to copy from. On the right, select the
   disk to copy to.

5. Click the Start button to begin the copying process. The progress
   bar at the bottom of the dialog box indicates how much information remains to be copied.

6. If you are working with a single drive, you will be prompted to
   swap source and target disks as the copy proceeds.

You will see the message "Copy Completed Successfully " when the program
has completed copying. Get ready to copy another disk, or click the Close
button to close the Copy Disk dialog box.

Copying Files and Folders

When you copy a file or a folder, you duplicate it in another location and
leave the original in place. In Windows, you can copy files and folders in
three ways.

Using Drag-and-Drop

To use the drag-and-drop method, both the source and the destination
folders must be open on the Desktop. Press and hold the Ctrl key while
holding down the left mouse button, and drag the file or folder from one
location to another. When the file or folder is in the correct place, release
the mouse button and then release the Ctrl key.

✖ w a r n i n g

Be sure to hold down Ctrl. If you do not, the file or folder will be moved rather
than copied.

Using the Edit Menu

The Edit menu in My Computer, Explorer, or any folder window provides a Copy and Paste feature. Follow these steps to use it:

1. Select the file or folder you want to copy.

2. Choose Edit ➤ Copy.

3. Find the destination file or folder and open it.

4. Choose Edit ➤ Paste.

You will see the name of the file in the destination folder.

▲ t i p

You can select multiple files or folders to be copied by holding down Ctrl and clicking them. If the files are contiguous, you can also use Shift to select files.

Using the Right Mouse Button

Right-clicking a file or a folder opens a pop-up menu that you can use to perform a number of functions, including copying. To copy using the right mouse button, follow these steps:

1. Locate the file or folder you want to copy, and right-click to open the pop-up menu. Select Copy.

2. Open the destination folder, click the right mouse button, and select Paste.

You will see the name of the file in the destination folder.

Creating New Folders

Sooner or later you will want to add a new folder to a disk or to another folder, and you can do so in Explorer. Follow these steps:

1. In Explorer, select the disk or folder in which you want to place a new folder.

2. Choose File ➤ New ➤ Folder.

Dd   date/time

A new folder is added to the disk or the folder you indicated with the name "New Folder" highlighted.

> **3.** Type a new folder name, something that will act as a reminder as to the files it contains, and press Enter.

You can also right-click in the blank part of the Windows Explorer file pane to open a pop-up menu from which you can choose New ➤ Folder.

▲ t i p

If you would rather bypass the Explorer altogether, you can create a new folder on the Desktop by clicking My Documents and then choosing File ➤ New ➤ Folder. Give the folder a new name, and then drag it to the Desktop.

Date/Time

 The clock that appears in the right corner of the Taskbar displays the system clock, which not only tells you the time, but also indicates the time and date associated with any files you create or modify.

To set the clock, follow these steps:

> **1.** Double-click the time in the Taskbar, or choose Start ➤ Settings ➤ Control Panel ➤ Date/Time to open the Date/Time Properties dialog box.
>
> **2.** Select the Date & Time tab to set the day, month, year, or current time.
>
> **3.** To change the time, either drag across the numbers you want to change beneath the clock and type the new time, or highlight the numbers and click the up and down arrows to increase or decrease the values.
>
> **4.** To change the date, click the drop-down arrow to select the month, use the up and down arrows to change the year, and click the appropriate day of the month.

▲ t i p

At any time, you can place the mouse pointer on the time in the Taskbar to display the complete date.

✔ **n o t e**

To vary the format of the date and time displayed in the Taskbar, select the Regional Settings applet in the Control Panel.

Deleting Files and Folders

You can delete a file or a folder in several ways. First, select the file or folder you want in My Computer or Windows Explorer, and then do one of the following:

▶ Choose File ➤ Delete. After you confirm that you want to delete the file or folder, Windows sends it to the Recycle Bin.

▶ Press the Delete key on the keyboard and verify that you want to delete the selected file or folder; Windows then sends it to the Recycle Bin.

▶ Right-click the file or folder to open the pop-up menu. Select Delete and then verify that you want to delete the selected file or folder. Off it goes to the Recycle Bin.

▶ Position the My Computer or Explorer window so that you can also see the Recycle Bin on the Desktop; then simply drag the selected file or folder to the Recycle Bin.

✔ **n o t e**

If you accidentally delete a file or folder, you can choose Edit ➤ Undo Delete or retrieve the file or folder manually from the Recycle Bin. You cannot retrieve a deleted file or folder if the Recycle Bin has been emptied since your last deletion.

▲ **t i p**

To delete a file without placing it in the Recycle Bin, select the file and then press Shift+Delete. You cannot recover the file if you do this. You will be asked to confirm the deletion.

Desktop

What you see on the screen when you first open Windows. If you are not using any of the Web-like features of the Active Desktop, you see the conventional Windows Desktop. Initially, it contains a set of icons arranged on the left, plus the Taskbar with the Start button across the bottom. As you work with Windows and load application programs, other objects such as dialog boxes and messages boxes are placed on the Desktop.

You can also change the appearance of the Desktop by right-clicking it and selecting Properties. This allows you to change display properties for the Desktop background and screen savers. You can also change the monitor type, as well as font types, sizes, and colors for objects on the screen.

Disk Space

To find out how much disk space a file or folder occupies, select it (hold down the Ctrl key to select more than one) in My Computer or Explorer. If the window's status bar is turned on in the View menu, the number of objects selected and the amount of disk space they occupy are displayed at the bottom of the window.

Alternately, you can choose File ➤ Properties or right-click a file or folder and select Properties. The General tab displays the amount of disk space or, in the case of a folder, its size plus the number of files or other folders it contains.

To see how much disk space remains on the entire disk, select the disk name in My Computer or Explorer and then choose File ➤ Properties or right-click and choose Properties. The Properties dialog box displays both the amount of used space and the amount of free space. The status bar of My Computer also displays the free space and capacity of a disk drive.

Display

 Controls how the objects on you screen—patterns, colors, fonts, sizes, and other elements—look. Choose Start ➤ Settings ➤ Control Panel ➤ Display to open the Display Properties dialog box. It has six tabs: Background, Screen Saver, Appearance, Effects, Web, and Settings.

▲ t i p
You can also open the Display Properties dialog box by right-clicking the Desktop and selecting Properties.

Background Tab

You can choose an HTML document or a picture to use as your Desktop background. In the Wallpaper box, select the background you want to use, or click Pattern to choose or modify the background pattern. You can also click the Browse button to locate a file or to go directly to a Web site to find the HTML document you are interested in using as a background.

To cover your entire Desktop with a small wallpaper image, select Tile from the Display box, or select Center if you prefer to see the image centered. Click the Apply button to see the effect of your changes before you exit the Display Properties dialog box, or click OK to accept the changes and close the dialog box.

Screen Saver Tab

A screen saver provides a constantly changing image on the screen to prevent a fixed image from being burned into the screen. A screen saver automatically appears after the computer is unused for a period of time. You can turn on, preview, and select a screen saver from the Screen Saver tab, which contains the following options:

Screen Saver Lists the available screen savers. Click the one you want to preview in the display box.

Settings Determines the speed and density of the pattern of the screen saver.

Preview Displays the screen saver in full-screen view.

To return to the dialog box, move the mouse or press any key.

Password Protected Requires a password for access beyond the screen saver. Windows will not clear the screen saver until the correct password is given.

Change Allows you to change the password. It is available only when Password Protected is enabled. You must be able to confirm the old password to change to a new password.

Wait Sets the amount of time before the screen saver is activated.

If you have a PC and monitor with built-in energy-saving features, click the Settings button to open the Power Management Properties dialog box. You

Dd display

can also access this dialog box directly from the Power Management applet in the Control Panel. You may not see all the options described here if your hardware does not support these power-saving features.

You can set the length of idle time after which you want Windows to turn off your monitor and your hard disk; time periods extend from After 1 Minute to Never, which effectively disables the power management features on your computer.

If you have a laptop that supports the feature, you can click the Hibernate tab to specify that your laptop goes into hibernation when you close the lid. When you put your computer into hibernation, everything in memory is saved to the hard disk so that when you turn your computer on again, all the applications and documents that were open when you closed the lid are reloaded.

Once you choose the appropriate settings for your system, you can save them as a named Power Scheme or, in other words, as a group of preset options. Click the Save As button in the top part of the Power Management Properties dialog box to do so.

Appearance Tab

The display window at the top of this tab shows how the major Windows elements, such as window borders, fonts, and colors, are currently configured. You can change all these elements using the following options:

Scheme Lists the preset schemes that change the appearance of windows, dialog boxes, and message boxes. You can select a scheme from the list or create your own. For example, the Evergreen 256 scheme displays window and box borders in green with a contrasting background.

Item Allows you to select a single item and customize its appearance. Depending on the item, you can change the size or the color.

Font Sets the font for the selected item, when appropriate. The following options are available:

Size Sets the point size.

Color Sets the color of the text.

B Boldfaces the text.

/ Italicizes the text.

Effects Tab

Lets you work with Desktop icons and certain visual effects. Use the Desktop Icons box at the top of this tab to select a new icon or return to the default icon for My Computer, My Documents, Network Neighborhood, and the full and empty Recycle Bin. You can also specify that your Desktop icons are hidden when the Desktop is viewed as a Web page.

You can also turn on or off the following visual effects: Use Large Icons, Show Icons Using all Possible Colors, Use Menu Animations, Smooth Edges of Screen Fonts, and Show Window Contents While Dragging.

Web Tab

Lets you select and organize Active Desktop elements. At the top of the tab is a representation of your Desktop, indicating the location of any Active Desktop elements. These same elements are listed in the box below. To add a new element such as a stock ticker or a weather map, click New to open the New Active Desktop Item dialog box. If you want to browse through Microsoft's Active Desktop Gallery on Microsoft's Web site for a component to add, click Yes. To select a different Web site, click No, and then enter the address, or URL, for the Web site, or click the Browse button to locate it. Be sure the *View my Active Desktop as a Web page* box is checked if you want your Desktop to look like a Web page.

Choose the Reset All button to restore all settings in the Web tab to their original default values.

Settings Tab

Allows you to vary the resolution and color palette that your monitor and display adapter card use. The Windows Setup program determines these settings, and most people never change them.

The following options are available:

Colors Establishes the color palettes that your monitor and display adapter support—either 16-color or 256-color for lower resolution monitors and High Color (16 bit) and True Color (24 bit) for higher resolutions.

Screen Area Sets the resolution of your monitor, in terms of pixels.

Click the Advanced button to open a dialog box specifically for your display adapter. In this dialog box, you will find tabs relating to the adapter card settings, your monitor, hardware graphics acceleration, and color management.

Documents

 Choosing Start ➤ Documents displays a list of all the documents you have created or edited recently. If you select a document from the list, Windows opens the document in the appropriate application, making this a quick way to continue working on an interrupted project.

Windows maintains this list of documents and preserves it between Windows sessions even if you shut down and restart your computer. The last 15 documents are preserved in this list, but some of them may look more like applications or folders than documents.

To clear the list of documents and start the list over, choose Start ➤ Settings ➤ Taskbar & Start Menu. Select the Start Menu Programs tab and click the Clear button. Once you do this, only one entry will remain in the list, the shortcut to the My Documents folder.

Drag and Drop

You can use drag and drop to move, copy, activate, or dispose of files and folders on the Desktop and in many accessory and application windows. Place the mouse pointer on a file, press the left button, and drag the file or folder to another disk or folder. Position the pointer over the destination and release the mouse button. The result depends on the file or folder being dragged and the destination:

▶ Dragging a file or folder to another folder on the same disk moves it (hold down the Ctrl key if you want to copy the file or folder).

▶ Dragging a file or folder to another disk copies it.

▶ Dragging a file to a shortcut printer icon on the Desktop prints the document.

▶ Dragging a file or folder to the Recycle Bin disposes of it.

E-Mail
→*See Outlook Express*

Entertainment

 Choose Start ➤ Programs ➤ Accessories ➤ Entertainment to access
all the Windows 98 multimedia tools including the CD Player, Media
Player, Sound Recorder, TV Viewer, and the Volume Control.

Explorer

The Windows Explorer (to use its full name) is *the* place to go when
working with files and folders in Windows 98. The Explorer lets you
look at your disks, folders, and files, in a variety of ways and helps you perform such tasks as copying, moving, renaming, and deleting files and folders, formatting floppy disks, and so on.

Explorer Menus

To access Explorer, choose Start ➤ Programs ➤ Windows Explorer, or right-
click the Start button and choose Explore. You may want to create a shortcut for the Explorer on the Desktop or in the Start menu itself since it is
used so often.

The Explorer menus give you access to all common functions. However, for some
menu selections to work, you may first have to select an appropriate object
in the main Explorer window, and the type of object you select determines
the available options. You may, therefore, not see all these options on any
given menu, and you may see some options not listed here. You will also find
similar menus in My Computer, the Recycle Bin, and Network Neighborhood.

File Menu
Displays basic file-management options. It allows you to do the following:

▶ Open a folder or file

▶ Explore the contents of a selected computer, disk, or folder

▶ Print a file or get a Quick View of the contents of a file (not shown
on the menu unless it is available)

33

- Set parameters for sharing a folder with other users

- Send a file to a floppy disk, as e-mail or a fax using Windows Messaging, to My Briefcase, or to another destination

- Create a new folder or a shortcut

- Make a shortcut to a file or folder

- Delete or rename a file or folder

- Display a file's properties

- Close a file or a folder

If you are working with the Printers folder, you will also see Capture Printer Port and End Capture options.

Edit Menu
Allows you to work with the contents of a folder or file. It allows you to do the following:

- Undo the previous action

- Cut, copy, and paste folders or files

- Paste a shortcut within a folder

- Select all files and folders

- Select all files except those already selected, which become deselected

View Menu
Allows you to change the window to include or exclude the toolbars, Status bar, and Explorer bar. You can choose how the files and folders are displayed:

- As a Web page

- With large icons or small icons

- In a list

- With details, describing the size and type of a file and the date modified

You can arrange icons by name, type of file or folder, size, or date created or last modified. You can also arrange icons into columns and rows. Refresh redisplays your screen. Folder Options lets you set defaults for how information is displayed in the main Explorer window, and Customize This Folder lets you change the appearance of the folder.

Go Menu
Lets you go back, forward, or up one level and gives fast access to certain Web sites and other Windows elements such as Mail, News, My Computer, Address Book, and Internet Call.

Favorites Menu
The Favorites menu is divided into two parts. You use the first part to manage your favorite Web sites with Add to Favorites and Organize Favorites, as well as those Web sites to which you subscribe with Manage Subscriptions and Update All Subscriptions. You use the second part for fast access to groups of Web sites with Channels, Links, and Software Updates.

Tools Menu
Gives you quick access to Find so that you can find Files or Folders, Computer, On the Internet, or People. You can also map a networked drive and disconnect a networked drive.

Help Menu
Provides access to the Windows Help system.

▲ t i p
Some functions available from the Explorer menus are also available as buttons on the toolbar.

Explorer Toolbar
The following buttons are available on the standard Explorer toolbar:

Back   Displays the item you last displayed. Click the small down-pointing arrow just to the right of this button to see a list of all the items you have displayed in this Explorer session. You can click an item to go to it directly, rather than clicking the Back button as many times as necessary.

Forward Displays the item you were viewing before you went back to the current item. Click the small down-pointing arrow just to the right of this button to display a list of items. Click an item to go to it directly.

 Up Moves up the directory tree in the left Explorer window, changing the contents displayed in the right window as it goes.

 Cut Moves the selected items to the Clipboard.

 Copy Duplicates selected items, placing their content on the Clipboard.

 Paste Transfers the contents of the Clipboard to a file or folder. A destination folder must already exist and be selected.

 Undo Cancels the previous action. The label changes depending on what you did last—for example, Undo Delete or Undo Copy.

 Delete Places the selected file or folder in the Recycle Bin.

 Properties Opens the Properties dialog box for the selected disk, file, or folder.

Views Changes the way information is displayed in the right-hand Explorer window. Click the small down-pointing arrow just to the right of this button to display a menu you can use to select the various displays. Alternatively, each time you click the Views button, the display cycles through these four views:

Large Icons Displays larger-sized icons representing the contents of the selected folder or disk.

Small Icons Displays smaller-sized icons in a horizontal, columnar list representing the contents of the selected folder or disk.

List Displays the contents as small icons, except in a vertical rather than horizontal orientation.

     Details   Displays the contents in a detailed list with additional information about the file size, file type, and modification date.

▲ **t i p**

In the Details view, you can change the column sizes by dragging the column break. You can also sort the Details view by clicking a column heading. It acts as a toggle switch: The first time you click, you'll see an ascending sort; the second time, a descending sort.

The Explorer also contains two other toolbars:

     Address   Displays the location of the item currently displayed by the Explorer. The arrow at the right end of the Address toolbar opens a drop-down list of items; select one to open it.

     Links   Displays a set of hyperlinks to various parts of Microsoft's Web site; you can also access these links from the Links selection in the Favorites menu.

▲ **t i p**

You can mix and match all these separate toolbars using the Toolbars, Status Bar, and Explorer Bar selections from the View menu.

You will also see a single status line across the bottom of the main Explorer window; it displays messages about your actions and lists information on disk storage space, including the number of items in a folder and the occupied and free disk space.

Explorer Window

When you run the Explorer, all items that make up your computer are listed in the left pane. Some objects have a plus sign (+) next to them, indicating that the object contains other objects that are not currently visible. To display the contents of such an item in the right pane, click the item, not the plus sign.

When you click the plus sign associated with an object, you display all the subelements, usually folders, in the left window, where they become part of the overall tree structure. The plus sign becomes a minus sign (-) when an object's contents are expanded. This tree structure is a graphical representation of how the files and folders on your system are related; the name of each folder appears just after its icon. If you have more files and folders than will fit in the Explorer window, use the scroll bars—one in the left pane and one in the right—to scroll the display up and down.

▲ **t i p**
To collapse everything, click the minus sign next to My Computer.

Customizing a Folder
You can change the appearance of a folder in two ways:

▶ You can add a background picture (in the same way that you can add wallpaper to your Desktop).

▶ You can create an HTML document and completely customize the appearance of the folder.

Choose View ➤ Customize This Folder to open the Customize This Folder Wizard with these options:

Create or Edit an HTML Document Lets you create an HTML (HyperText Markup Language) document in three steps:

1. Open the editor and create the HTML document.
2. Save the document.
3. Close the editor.

Choose a Background Picture Lets you select a picture that will be displayed as wallpaper when you open this folder.

Remove Customization Lets you return this folder to its original look and feel.

Selecting a Drive and Choosing a File or a Folder
When you open the Explorer, all the disks and folders available on your computer are displayed in the left pane. The right pane displays the contents of

the disk or folder you selected on the left. Follow these steps to find a file or a folder:

1. Scroll up and down using the left scroll bar. On the left, you can see all the disks on your computer, plus those that are shared on your network, and all the folders within each disk. On the right, you will see all the folders and files within the selected disk or folder.

2. If the drive you want is not visible, you may have to expand the My Computer icon by clicking its plus sign. Normally, you will be able to see a floppy disk and at least one hard disk.

3. Click a disk or folder in the left pane to display its contents in the right pane; when a folder is selected, its icon changes from a closed folder to an open one. If the folder you select contains other folders, they will be listed in the right pane, followed by any files within the folder.

4. Once you find the file or folder you want, open it and get to work.

✔ n o t e

One of the beauties of Explorer is the ability to drag a file or a folder from the right pane to any object in the left pane. If you do this within the same disk drive, you *move* the object to the new location. If you press Ctrl while dragging or you drag to an object outside the current disk, you *copy* the object you are dragging.

▲ t i p

When you right-click a file, the pop-up menu duplicates many functions found in the File and Edit menus, giving you the ability to open the file, send a copy as a fax or as e-mail or to another disk, cut or copy it, create a shortcut for it, delete or rename it, or display the Properties dialog box for it. Right-clicking a folder gives you the same options plus Explore (which displays its contents on the right), Find (which opens the Find dialog box), and Sharing (which sets parameters for allowing the folder to be shared). Right-clicking a disk icon also allows you to format a disk.

Favorites

 Contains selections you can use to track your favorite Web sites. You can open your favorite Web sites from many places within

Ff favorites

Windows 98. You can choose Start ➤ Favorites, or you can use the Favorites menu in Windows Explorer, My Computer, Internet Explorer, Network Neighborhood, and Control Panel; even the Recycle Bin has a Favorites menu.

Add to Favorites

Choose Favorites ➤ Add to Favorites to bookmark a Web site so that you can find it again quickly and easily. Once you place the address, or URL, for the site in this list, you can revisit the site simply by selecting it from the Favorites menu; the result is the same as if you had typed the whole URL into the Address toolbar and pressed Enter. You can also display your Favorites menu from the Explorer Bar; choose View ➤ Explorer Bar ➤ Favorites.

Organize Favorites

Choose Favorites ➤ Organize Favorites to group your Web sites into an arrangement that makes sense to you; a single long list is certainly not the most efficient organization.

The Organize Favorites dialog box contains the following buttons:

Move   Lets you reorganize the folders within your Favorites folder.

Rename   Lets you change the name of the selected item.

Delete   Removes the selected item.

Open   Displays the selected folder in a new Explorer window.

Click the Create New Folder button if you want to make a brand-new folder for some of your favorite Web sites.

Subscribing to a Web Site

In addition to visiting Web sites in the normal way with Internet Explorer, you can also subscribe to a Web site. A subscription is a mechanism that Internet Explorer uses to check for new or updated content on a Web site without your involvement.

When you subscribe to one of the Web sites on your Favorites menu, Internet Explorer automatically checks the site for new content on a schedule that you specify. You can also choose to be notified when it finds updated content or to have Internet Explorer automatically download and store the new material on your hard disk so that you can look at it offline.

To create a new subscription, open the page, choose Favorites ➤ Add to Favorites to open the Add Favorite dialog box, and then choose one of these options:

▶   Yes, but only tell me when this page is updated

▶   Yes, notify me of updates and download the page for offline viewing

And to specify the delivery, schedule, and notification options, click the Customize button to open the Web Site Subscription Wizard. You can specify that the Web site is visited daily, weekly, monthly, or when the Update All Subscriptions option is next invoked from the Favorites menu.

To change these subscription settings later, choose Favorites ➤ Manage Subscriptions, right-click the subscription you want to look at or change, and then select Properties.

Find

Windows 98 adds several powerful items to the Find menu, which now includes options for finding files and folders, a computer, information on the Internet, or people. Choose Start ➤ Find and select an option, or choose Tools ➤ Find in Explorer.

Find Files or Folders

To find a file or folder, you can either use My Computer or Explorer to scan the disks yourself, or you can use the Find command to have Windows 98 conduct the search for you. To use the Find command, choose Start ➤ Find ➤ Files or Folders, or in Explorer, choose Tools ➤ Find ➤ Files or Folders.

In the Find: All Files dialog box, you will see three tabs: Name & Location, Date, and Advanced.

Name & Location Tab
Contains the following options:

Named   Displays the name of the file or folder for which you're searching. Click the down arrow to display a list of your most recent searches.

Containing Text   Lets you specify any text that you want to locate.

Ff find

Look In Tells Windows to search a specific path for the file or folder. Click the down arrow to display a list of the disks and folders on your computer.

Browse Lets you look through the available disks and folders to find the one you want.

Include Subfolders Searches sublevels of folders as well as the level you specified.

Date Tab
Contains the following options:

All Files Searches all files in the specified path for the desired file or folder.

Find All Files Restricts the search to files created, last accessed, or modified between two specified dates, during the previous number of months, or during the previous number of days.

Advanced Tab
Contains the following options:

Of Type Searches for a specific type of file. Click the down arrow to display a list of registered types.

Size Is Restricts the search for files to At Least or At Most (selected by the first down arrow) the number of kilobytes specified (typed or entered using the arrow keys).

Enter the Find specifications you want, and then select one of the following buttons:

Find Now Starts the search.

Stop Ends the search.

New Search Allows you to enter new search criteria.

To save a search, including its parameters, choose File ➤ Save Search. To save the results of a search, choose Options ➤ Save Results. To make a search case-sensitive, choose Options ➤ Case Sensitive.

Find a Computer

To locate a computer on your network using the Find command in either the Start menu or Explorer, follow these steps:

1. Chose Start ➤ Find ➤ Computer, or in Explorer, choose Tools ➤ Find ➤ Computer to open the Find: Computer dialog box.

2. Enter the computer name or select it from a list of previous searches by clicking the Named down arrow.

3. Click Find Now to activate the search. Stop terminates the search, and New Search allows you to enter the criteria for a new computer search.

Find on the Internet

The Find menu's On the Internet option uses Internet Explorer to connect to the Microsoft Web site. This single Web site gives you access to some of the most powerful and popular search engines on the Internet, including Infoseek, AOL NetFind, Lycos, Excite, and Yahoo. Each works slightly differently, and each has strengths and weaknesses.

And if that isn't enough, you can also use one of the other sites in the categories of General Search, Guides, White Pages, Newsgroups, Chat Guides, Specialty, or International. If you can't find what you are looking for using one of these search engines, what you are looking for doesn't want to be found.

Find People

The Find menu's People option lets you search public LDAP (Lightweight Directory Access Protocol) directories on the Internet such as Bigfoot (www.bigfoot.com), Four11 (www.four11.com), and WhoWhere? (www.whowhere.com) for particular information. Here are the steps:

1. Choose Start ➤ Find ➤ People, or in Explorer, choose Tools ➤ Find ➤ People to open the Find People dialog box.

2. In the Look In list, select the name of the directory service you want to use.

3.   Type the information on the person you are looking for, usually just the first name followed by the last name, and then click Find Now.

The results of a search may vary depending on which of the services you use, but you will normally see a long list of names with different e-mail addresses. It is then up to you to decide which of those names is actually the person you want to contact.

Folder Options

In Explorer, choose View ➤ Folder Options to open the Folder Options dialog box, in which you specify how your folders will look and work. You can also choose Start ➤ Settings ➤ Folder Options if you prefer. The Folder Options dialog box contains three tabs: General, View, and File Types. When you open the Folder Options dialog box in My Computer, Network Neighborhood, and the Recycle Bin, you will see two tabs: General and View.

General Tab
Defines how the following systemwide settings work on your computer:

Web Style   Specifies that your folders work with a single click just like the Web. Icon names will be underlined, and the normal arrow-shaped mouse pointer will turn into a hand as it passes over the icon.

Classic Style   Specifies that your folders behave in the traditional Windows way. Click once to select an item; double-click to open or run an item.

Custom, Based on Settings You Choose   Specifies that you want to choose your own configuration. Click the Settings button to set these preferences.

View Tab
Controls advanced settings for files and folders. The Folder Views box contains two options you can use to make all the folders on your system look and work in the same way:

Like Current Folder   Uses the current settings in effect in the View menu (except for the toolbar settings) on all folders on your computer.

Reset All Folders   Uses the original View menu settings in effect when the program was first installed.

The Advanced Settings box contains a set of checkboxes for certain display options, such as how to treat hidden files, whether file attributes are shown in the Details view, and so on. Check the box to turn that option on, and clear the box to turn it off again. Click the Restore Defaults button to put everything back into its original state.

File Types Tab

Displays all the file types currently registered with Windows; this is how Windows knows which program to use to open specific data files. When you select a file type in the list, the File Type Details box displays a short summary of which file name extension belongs to that type, its MIME (Multipurpose Internet Mail Extensions) content type, and the name of the program used to open it.

To change or delete one of the existing types, select it in the Registered File Types box, and then choose Edit or Remove. Click the New Type button to register a new file type with Windows. Here are the steps:

1. Click the New Type button to open the Add New File Type dialog box.

2. In the Description of Type field, enter a short text description along the lines of the other entries used, such as Active Streaming File Format.

3. Type the file name extension in the Associated Extension field.

4. Select an existing MIME Content_Type from the drop-down list, or enter a new MIME type.

5. Click the New button, and in the Actions field, enter the operation you want to perform; common operations are Open (to open the file) and Print. Then, in the *Application used to perform action* field, enter the full path and file name of the application you want to associate with this file type. Click OK when you are done.

6. Click OK to return to the File Types tab in the Folder Options dialog box.

Fonts

The styles of type used when Windows displays or prints text. Windows maintains a library of fonts that all applications that run under it use. Choose Start ➤ Settings ➤ Control Panel ➤ Fonts to open the Fonts folder, which displays all the fonts installed on your computer. Windows applications primarily use two types of fonts:

▶ TrueType fonts (represented by a pair of *T*s in the icon)

▶ Adobe fonts (represented by an *A* in the icon), which are bitmapped or vector fonts

In addition to the standard Large Icons, List, and Details views found in the View menu of the Fonts folder, there is a unique and quite useful view for fonts called List Fonts by Similarity. Clicking the Similarity button on the toolbar displays the same view. This shows the fonts that are reasonably alike, which can be handy if you know approximately how the font should look and want to see variations. Another useful and unique option in the View menu is View ➤ Hide Variations. If you have a lot of fonts, this option helps reduce the selection to only the main fonts by hiding bold, italics, and so on.

Fonts Used in Windows 98

The defaults for the size and type of fonts used in the Windows 98 windows and dialog boxes are set in the Display Properties dialog box. You can vary the font and size for text objects and for menus, message boxes, and title bars.

Right-click the Desktop and choose Properties from the pop-up menu to open the Display Properties dialog box, or choose Start ➤ Settings ➤ Control Panel ➤ Display. You use the Appearance and Settings tabs to control the size of fonts on the screen and the size and typeface of fonts for selected objects on the screen.

Adding a New Font to Your Computer

If you have acquired some new fonts, you can add them to those that come with Windows 98 by following these steps:

1. Choose Start ➤ Settings ➤ Control Panel ➤ Fonts to open the Fonts folder.

2. Choose File ➤ Install New Font to open the Add Fonts dialog box.

3. Select the drive and then select the folder that contains the new font.

4. Click the font you want to add. Hold down the Ctrl key and then click to select more than one font.

Displaying and Printing Font Samples

Once you have collected a large number of fonts, remembering what each one looks like can be difficult. Fortunately, the Windows 98 Font Viewer can help. To use it, follow these steps:

1. Open the Fonts folder.

2. Select any icon in the folder to open that font in the Font Viewer. Open additional Font Viewer windows if you want to compare two or more fonts.

3. To print an example of the font, click the Print button in the Font Viewer; alternatively, right-click the font in the Fonts folder and select Print from the pop-up menu.

Formatting Disks

Format...   Unless you purchase formatted disks, you must format a floppy disk before you can use it the first time. Formatting a new disk places information on the disk that Windows needs to be able to read and write files and folders to and from the disk. Formatting a used disk erases all the original information it contained and turns it into a blank disk, so be sure that you are formatting the right disk.

To format a floppy disk, follow these steps:

1. Place the floppy disk you want to format in the disk drive.

2. From My Computer, select the disk drive containing the disk for formatting and then choose File ➤ Format to open the Format dialog box. You can also right-click the disk drive in My Computer or Explorer.

3. Enter or confirm the following specifications:

Capacity Specifies the maximum amount of data that the disk can hold. To select a different capacity, click the down arrow and then select an option from the list.

Format Type Controls the type of formatting. Choose Quick (erase) if the disk contains no bad sectors. Choose Full if you want Windows to check for bad sectors and attempt to repair them. Choose Copy System Files Only to produce a disk that you can use to boot the system using the specified drive (the disk will not be formatted; only system files will be copied to the disk).

Label Allows you to place a name on a disk so that it can be more easily identified in the future.

No Label Places no name on the disk and removes any that was previously there.

Display Summary When Finished Displays a short report describing the space available on the disk and listing any bad sectors.

Copy System Files Copies system files to the disk after formatting so that it can be used for booting.

4. Click the Start button when you are ready to begin formatting the floppy disk. Clicking Close closes the dialog box without saving the specifications you have made.

FrontPage Express

A quick-and-easy Web-page editor you can use to create or customize your own Web pages without having to learn the details of HyperText Markup Language (HTML). You can edit Web-page elements by selecting them in the main FrontPage Express window and then using a toolbar button or menu selection to apply formatting and alignment. You can also:

- Apply HTML tags directly from the toolbar.

- Select text, graphics, audio, and video using the mouse or the keyboard.

- Open existing Web pages from the Internet or from your own corporate intranet.

- Save pages back to the Web using the Web Publishing Wizard or to a file for uploading later.

- Insert watermarks, ActiveX controls, Microsoft PowerPoint animations, and Java applets to extend the power of your Web pages.

- Use advanced features such as tables, forms, and marquees for presentation and data collection.

Choose Start ➤ Programs ➤ Internet Explorer ➤ FrontPage Express to open the program.

Games

Windows 98 includes four games: FreeCell, Hearts, Minesweeper, and that addictive timewaster, Solitaire. You can play Hearts over the network with other players. To get to the games, choose Start ➤ Programs ➤ Accessories ➤ Games, and then click the game you want to play. If you get stuck, click Help for instructions on how to play.

Go
→*See Internet Explorer*

Hardware
→*See Add New Hardware*

Help

Windows 98 contains an extensive help system that provides you with online assistance at almost any time. You can use the main Windows 98 Help System to gain access to a huge amount of information, you can use Windows 98 Troubleshooters to diagnose and isolate a problem relating to specific hardware or software, and you can use Web Help to connect directly to Microsoft's Web site to look for program updates.

Windows Help System

Choose Start ➤ Help to open the main Windows 98 Help System dialog box, which has three tabs:

Contents   Lists the main categories in the Help system itself and a general overview of Windows 98. Each category is a folder containing subjects or other categories. If you open a folder, you will see the subjects contained within the one category. If you open a subject, you will see the Help information for that specific subject.

Index   Lists all the subjects in the Help system in one giant alphabetic list. Type the first few letters of the word you're looking for in the text box at the top of this tab, and the list box will automatically scroll to the subject closest in spelling to what you have typed. Or you can scroll to it yourself by using the scroll bars on the right of the display box. When you get to the subject you want, select it and click Display.

Search   Allows you to find specific words or phrases contained within a Help topic. To do this, Windows must create a database containing words used throughout the Help system. When you click the Search tab for the first time, the Search Setup Wizard creates this database. You can then use the Search tab to find the specific word or phrase you want.

When a Help topic is displayed, you may see a link icon. Click it to open the specific application, dialog box, or other element under discussion. When you close the application, you return to the same place in the Help System.

Using the Built-In Troubleshooters

Windows 98 extends the usual concepts of the Help system to include a set of built-in technical support troubleshooters you can use to help diagnose and isolate certain problems. There are two ways to find the right Troubleshooter and start it running on your system:

▶   You can choose Start ➤ Help to open the Windows 98 Help System. Select the Contents tab, select the Troubleshooting topic, and then open Windows 98 Troubleshooters. Choose the appropriate Troubleshooter from the list and follow the directions on the screen.

> ▶ Alternatively, you can start a Troubleshooter directly from a page
> of Help information. As you read through the information the
> page contains, you will come across a link to a Troubleshooter;
> click the link to start the Troubleshooter.

Once the Troubleshooter starts, click the Hide button on the Help toolbar to
close the left pane. Be sure to follow all the steps the Troubleshooter suggests.

Troubleshooters are available for problems encountered with networking, printing, startup and shutdown, hardware such as modems, and
procedures such as dial-up networking and connecting to the Microsoft
Network.

Getting Web Help

Click the Web Help button on the Help System toolbar to connect to a
Microsoft site to look for updated versions of programs and device drivers.
You then select what you want to install; perhaps more important, you can
also uninstall a program or a device driver that is causing you problems.

▲ t i p

All the popular Windows applications also contain a Help menu you can use to
display information specific to that program.

Help in a Dialog Box

Context-sensitive Help is also available in certain dialog boxes. You may see
a Help button on a dialog box; click it to see information specific to that
dialog box.

Other dialog boxes have a Help button in the upper-right corner (look for
the button with a question mark on it) next to the Close button. Click this
Help button and the question mark jumps onto the cursor; move the cursor
to the entry that you want help with and click again. A small window containing the help text opens; click the mouse to close this window when
you are done.

▲ t i p

You can also right-click certain objects to open a small menu containing the
single selection What's This. Click What's This to display a small window of help
text for that object.

Internet

 In Windows 98, you can view or change the configuration options relating to the Internet in two ways:

▶   Via your connection to the Internet

▶   In Internet Explorer

To open the Internet Options dialog box, choose Start ➤ Connections ➤ Control Panel ➤ Internet, or open Internet Explorer and choose View ➤ Internet Options. The Internet Options dialog box has six tabs.

General Tab

Contains these groups of settings:

Home Page   Lets you choose which Web page opens each time you connect to the Internet. The home page is the first Web page you see when you start Internet Explorer. Click Use Current to make the current page your home page, click Use Default to return to the default setting, and click Use Blank to start each Internet session with a blank screen. To use a different Web page as your home page, type the URL in the Address box.

Temporary Internet Files   Lets you manage those Web pages that are stored on your hard disk for fast offline access. If these files are occupying too much hard-disk space, click the Delete Files button to remove them. To control how these files are stored on your hard disk, click Settings to open the Settings dialog box. Click the option that applies to when you want Internet Explorer to check for newer versions of these stored Web pages. You can use the slider to specify how much hard-disk space is given over to these temporary Internet files. Click Move Folder if you want to use a different folder to hold your temporary Internet files; you must remember to restart your computer after making this change so that the new folder is used in place of the default. Click View Files to open an Explorer window listing all the Web and graphics files in the folder, or click View Objects to open an Explorer window listing all the other Web-related files such as ActiveX controls and Java-related files.

History   Contains a list of the links you have visited so that you can
return to them quickly and easily. You can specify the number of days
you want to keep pages in the History folder; if you are running low on
hard-disk space, consider reducing this number. To delete all the information currently in the History folder, click the Clear History button.

Colors   Lets you choose which colors are used as background, links,
and text on those Web pages for which the original author did not specify colors. By default, the Use Windows Colors option is selected.

▲ t i p
You can always change the Windows colors. In Control Panel, click Display and then
select the Appearance tab.

Fonts   Lets you specify the font style and text size to use on those
Web pages for which the original author did not make a specification.

Languages   Lets you choose the character set to use on those Web
pages that offer content in more than one language. English is rapidly
becoming the most common language in use on the Internet, so you
may not use this option often.

Accessibility   Lets you choose how certain information is displayed
in Internet Explorer, including font styles, colors, and text size. You can
also specify that your own style sheet is used.

Security Tab

Lets you specify the overall security level for each of four zones. Each zone
has its own default security restrictions that tell Internet Explorer how to
manage dynamic Web-page content such as ActiveX controls and Java
applets. The zones are:

Local Intranet   Sites you can access on your corporate intranet; security is set to medium.

Trusted Sites   Web sites you have a high degree of confidence will
not send you potentially damaging content; security is set to low.

Internet Sites you visit that are not in one of the other categories; security is set to medium.

Restricted Sites Sites that you visit but do not trust; security is set to high.

To change the current security level of a zone, select it from the list box, and then click the new security level you want to use:

High Excludes any content capable of damaging your system. This is the most secure setting.

Medium Opens a warning dialog box in Internet Explorer before running ActiveX or Java applets on your system. This is a moderately secure setting that is good for everyday use.

Low Does not issue any warning but runs the ActiveX or Java applet automatically. This is the least secure setting.

Custom Lets you create your own security settings. To look at or change these advanced settings, click the Settings button to open the Security Settings dialog box. You can individually configure how you want to manage certain categories, such as ActiveX controls and plug-ins, Java applets, scripting, file and font downloads, and user authentication.

Content Tab

Contains settings you can use to restrict access to sites and specify how you want to manage digital certificates:

Content Adviser Lets you control access to certain sites on the Internet and is particularly useful if children have access to the computer. Click Settings to establish a password, and then click OK to open the Content Advisor dialog box. Use the tabs in this dialog box to establish the level of content you will allow users to view:

Ratings Lets you use a set of ratings developed by the Recreational Software Advisory Council (RSAC) for language, nudity, sex, and violence. Select one of these categories, and then adjust the slider to specify the level of content you will allow.

General   Specifies whether people using this computer can view material that has not been rated; users may see some objectionable material if the Web site has not used the RSAC rating system. You can also opt to have the Supervisor enter a password so that users can view Web pages that may contain objectionable material. You can click the Change Password button to change the Supervisor password; remember that you have to know the current Supervisor password before you can change it.

Advanced   Lets you look at or modify the list of organizations providing ratings services.

Certificates   Lets you manage digital certificates used with certain client authentication servers. Click Personal to view the personal digital certificates installed on this system, click Authorities to list the security certificates installed on your system, or click Publishers to designate a particular software publisher as a trustworthy publisher. This means that Windows 98 applications can download, install, and use software from these agencies without asking for your permission first.

Personal Information   Lets you look at or change your own personal profile; this information is sent to any Web sites that request information when you visit their site. Click Edit Profile to review the current information:

> Personal
>
> Home
>
> Business
>
> Other
>
> NetMeeting
>
> Digital IDs

Click Reset Sharing to clear the list of sites you previously allowed to access your personal information without asking your permission first. Microsoft Wallet gives you a secure place to store credit card and other information you might need for Internet shopping.

Connection Tab

Allows you to specify how your system connects to the Internet:

Connection   Lets you specify whether your system will connect to the Internet via your corporate network or by modem. Click the Connect button to run the Connection Wizard and set up a connection to an Internet service provider (ISP). (See the Connection Wizard entry earlier in this book for complete details.) If you use a modem, click the Settings button to open the Dial-Up Settings dialog box where you can specify all aspects of the phone connection to your ISP.

Proxy Server   Lets you access the Internet via a proxy server system connected to your corporate intranet. A proxy server is a security system designed to monitor and control the flow of information between your intranet and the Internet. Click the Advanced button to specify detailed proxy-server configuration information; see your system administrator for more details on these settings.

Automatic Configuration   Lets your network system administrator configure your copy of Internet Explorer automatically. Click the Configure button to open the Automatic Configuration dialog box and enter the address of this configuration information.

Programs Tab

Lets you set your default program choices for e-mail, newsgroup reader, and so on and specify whether Internet Explorer should check to see if it is configured as the default browser:

Messaging   Lets you choose which application programs are used for mail, news, and Internet calls.

Personal Information   Lets you choose which application programs are used for calendar functions and for your contact list.

Finally, you can specify that Internet Explorer check to see if it is configured as the default browser on your system each time it starts running.

Advanced Tab

Lets you look at or change a number of settings that control much of Internet Explorer's behavior, including accessibility, browsing, multimedia, security, the

Java environment, printing and searching, and the Internet Explorer toolbar and how HTTP 1.1 settings are interpreted. Click a checkbox to turn an option on; clear the checkbox to turn the option off.

Changes you make here stay in effect until you change them again, until you download an automatic configuration file, or until you click the Restore Defaults button, which returns the settings on the Advanced tab to their original values.

Internet Connection Wizard

→ *See Connection Wizard*

Internet Explorer

 The application that displays Web pages from the Internet or from your corporate intranet. In many ways, Internet Explorer resembles Windows Explorer; it is a *viewer* that presents information in a structured way. Internet Explorer is an easy-to-use program that hides a large part of the complexity of the Internet and Internet operations.

You can start Internet Explorer in several ways:

▶   Choose Start ➤ Programs ➤ Internet Explorer ➤ Internet Explorer

▶   Click the Internet Explorer icon on the Desktop

▶   Open an Internet file from inside Windows Explorer or My Computer

▶   Enter an Internet address in the Browse dialog box

▶   Open an Internet address from within an Outlook Express e-mail message

▶   Choose Go ➤ Home Page in Windows Explorer, My Computer, or any other application that has a Go menu

Internet Explorer Toolbars

Three toolbars—Standard, Links, and Address—contain buttons that act as shortcuts to many items in the program's menus, and the Explorer bar, which is actually a special pane in the Internet Explorer main window, contains tools to help you navigate the Internet quickly and easily.

Standard Toolbar

Contains buttons you can use as shortcuts to some of the most often used Internet Explorer menu items:

 Back Displays the page you last displayed. Click the small down-pointing arrow just to the right of this button to see a list of all the items you have displayed in this Internet Explorer session. You can click an item to go to it directly, rather than clicking the Back button as many times as necessary.

 Forward Displays the page you were viewing before you went back to the current item. And just like the Back button, when you click the small down-pointing arrow just to the right of this button, you can display a list of items. Click an item to go to it directly.

 Stop Cancels the downloading of the current page.

 Refresh Updates the current page by downloading it again.

 Home Opens your home page, the Web page you see when you start Internet Explorer.

 Search Opens the Explorer Bar on the left side of the Internet Explorer window and displays the search options.

 Favorites Opens the Explorer Bar on the left side of the Internet Explorer window and displays the contents of your Favorites menu.

 History Opens the Explorer Bar and displays the contents of your History folder.

 Channels Opens the Explorer Bar and displays your channels.

Fullscreen Toggles Internet Explorer between full-screen or Channel View mode.

Mail Opens your default e-mail program.

Print   Prints the current Web page.

 Edit   Opens the current page in your Web-page editor, usually FrontPage Express.

Links Toolbar

All buttons on the Links toolbar are links to different parts of Microsoft's Web site; you can also access these links by choosing Favorites ➤ Links. Microsoft does an excellent job of keeping the information at these links up-to-date, so you will probably see something different each time you visit.

Address Toolbar

Shows the location of the Web page currently being displayed in the main Internet Explorer window; this may be a URL on the Internet, a URL on your intranet, or a file on your hard disk. To go to another Web site, enter its URL in the Address toolbar and press Enter.

▲ t i p

When you start to type in an address that you have previously entered, Internet Explorer's AutoComplete feature recognizes the URL and completes the entry for you.

Clicking the arrow at the right side of the Address toolbar opens a drop-down list of addresses you have previously entered using the Address toolbar; to open one, select it.

Explorer Bar

When you click the Search, Favorites, History, or Channels buttons on the main Internet Explorer toolbar or select one of these commands by choosing View ➤ Explorer Bar, the Explorer Bar appears as a special pane on the left side of the main Internet Explorer window. The information that this pane displays depends on which toolbar buttons you clicked. You can now make choices from the information in the left pane and see the results in the pane to the right.

To close the Explorer Bar, choose View ➤ Explorer Bar ➤ None, or click the
appropriate toolbar button a second time.

Internet Explorer Menus

You can use the buttons on the Internet Explorer toolbars, or you can use
menu items to get the job done. The Internet Explorer menus give you
access to all the common functions; however, for some menu items to
work, you may first have to select an appropriate object in the main Internet Explorer window. The options that become available depend on the
type of object you select.

File Menu

Displays basic file and URL management options and allows you to open a file
by specifying a name and URL or location. You can save or print the current
file, send the current page or its URL as an e-mail message, or create a Desktop
shortcut to it. You can also look at the properties for the current object, choose
to work offline, or go directly to a Web site you visited earlier in this session.

Edit Menu

In addition to the items found in any Windows Edit menu, the Internet
Explorer Edit menu includes Page, which opens the current page in the Front-
Page Express editor and searches for specific characters on the current page.

View Menu

Lets you hide or display all Internet Explorer toolbars and the Explorer Bar,
change the size or style of the fonts, cancel the downloading of the current
Web page, reload the current Web page, display the current Web page as
HTML source code, switch to full-screen mode, and look at or change any
setting in the Internet Options dialog box.

Go Menu

Lets you go back, forward, or up one level, as well as giving fast access to
certain Web sites and other Windows 98 elements such as Mail, News,
My Computer, Address Book, and Internet Call.

Favorites Menu

This menu is divided into two parts. You use the first part to manage your
favorite Web sites with Add to Favorites and Organize Favorites, as well as

those Web sites to which you subscribe with Manage Subscriptions and Update All Subscriptions. You use the second part for fast access to groups of Web sites with Channels, Links, and Software Updates.

▲ t i p
The Internet Explorer logo, shown at the right end of the menu bar, is animated when Internet Explorer is sending or receiving information; you can click this logo to go to the Microsoft's web site.

Help Menu
Gives you access to the Internet Explorer Help system through Contents and Index, lets you check for a newer version of Internet Explorer available through Product Updates, guides you through an online tutorial with Web Tutorial, and helps locate information on technical problems with Online Support.

When you choose Help ➤ Microsoft on the Web, the items on the submenu are actually links to different parts of the Microsoft Web site, including:

Free Stuff   Locates Internet Explorer program updates, free stuff, and add-on programs.

Get Faster Internet Access   Displays information about ISDN (Integrated Services Digital Network) service.

Frequently Asked Questions   Answers the most commonly asked questions about Internet Explorer.

Internet Start Page   Opens your home page.

Send Feedback   Lets you send your opinions right to Microsoft.

Best of the Web   Opens Microsoft's Exploring page, which contains a variety of links to useful and interesting sites. This is equivalent to clicking the Best of the Web button on the Internet Explorer Links toolbar.

Search the Web   Opens the same Web site as choosing Go ➤ Search the Web.

Microsoft Home Page   Opens Microsoft's Web site.

Internet Explorer Window

The major part of the Internet Explorer window consists of the document window where Web pages are displayed. As you move the mouse cursor around the page, it turns into a small hand whenever it passes over a link to another page. The page may be on the same Web site or on an entirely different Web site; simply click the link to open the new page.

The last line of the Internet Explorer main window holds the Status bar, which displays information about the current state of Internet Explorer. Icons you might see at the right end of the Status bar include a padlock, indicating you are connected to a secure Web site, and a network cable with a red X superimposed on top, indicating that you are working offline.

You can right-click many of the objects displayed in the main Internet Explorer window to open a pop-up menu. The choices on the pop-up menu depend on the type of object you choose:

- If you right-click a blank part of the window, the pop-up menu contains items relevant to the complete page. You can open the next or the previous page, add the current page to your Favorites menu, display the page as HTML source code, and so on. If the page contains a background image, you can save the image to a file or use it as your Desktop wallpaper.

- If you right-click a link, the pop-up menu lets you open the link; save, print, or copy the address information to the Clipboard; and add the address to your Favorites menu.

- If you right-click a graphic, the pop-up menu lets you save the image in a file, use the image as your Desktop wallpaper, or copy the image to the Clipboard.

- If you right-click selected text, you can copy the text to the Clipboard or print the text.

Configuring Internet Explorer

To view or set the many configuration options for Internet Explorer, choose View ➤ Internet Options to open the Internet Options dialog box. Or you can choose Start ➤ Connections ➤ Control Panel ➤ Internet. The Internet Options dialog box has six tabs. For a complete discussion of all the settings on these tabs, see the Internet entry earlier in this book.

Returning to Your Favorite Pages

One of the most common problems associated with using the Internet is finding your way back to something, a Web page or even a complete Web site, that you want to revisit.

▲ **t i p**

If you want to return to a Web site you visited during your current Internet Explorer session, click the Back and Forward buttons on the Internet Explorer toolbar, or choose Go ➤ Back and Go ➤ Forward. You will also see the names of the sites you have most recently accessed listed in the Internet Explorer File menu; simply select the name to open the site. Closing Internet Explorer removes these items from the File menu.

But by far the easiest way to keep track of interesting Web sites is to add them to your list of favorite sites.

Add to Favorites

When you want to bookmark a Web site so that you can find it again quickly and easily, choose Favorites ➤ Add to Favorites to open the Add Favorite dialog box.

Once you place the address or URL for the site in this list, you can revisit the site simply by selecting it from the Favorites menu; the result is the same as if you had typed the whole URL into the Address toolbar and pressed Enter. You can also display your Favorites menu from the Explorer bar; simply click the Favorites button. In addition, you can choose View ➤ Explorer Bar ➤ Favorites. To close the Favorites folder, click the Close button in the top right corner, or click the Favorites button on the toolbar a second time.

Organize Favorites

Keeping a single long list is certainly not the best way to organize your favorites. To group Web sites in some sort of arrangement that makes sense to you, choose Favorites ➤ Organize Favorites to open the Organize Favorites dialog box, which contains the following buttons:

> **Move**   Lets you reorganize the folders within your Favorites folder. You can also move any item within the Organize Favorites dialog box by dragging it to a different folder. Or you can right-click a favorite, choose Cut from the pop-up menu, browse your way to the folder

63

where you want to move the favorite, right-click inside that folder, and choose Paste from the pop-up menu there.

Rename   Lets you change the name of the selected item. You can also press F2 to edit the name.

Delete   Removes the selected item.

Open   Displays the selected folder in a new Explorer window. Alternatively, you can right-click and choose Open. To look at the contents of a folder, simply double-click it.

Click the Create New Folder button if you want to make a brand-new folder for some of your favorites Web sites. When you create a new folder within your Favorites folder, you also create a submenu on the Favorites menu for that same folder.

▲ t i p

You can open your favorite Web sites from many places within Windows 98. You can choose Start ➤ Favorites, or you can use the Favorites menu in Windows Explorer, My Computer, Internet Explorer, Network Neighborhood, and Control Panel; even the Recycle Bin has a Favorites menu.

Going Back with History

Once you access a Web site using Internet Explorer, its address (or URL) is stored in your History folder. You can use this list of all the sites you have visited to return to any one of them quickly and easily.

▲ t i p

When several people use the same computer by logging on with different user names and passwords, Internet Explorer creates separate History folders for each of them.

To access the information in your History folder, choose View ➤ Explorer Bar ➤ History, or click the History button on the Internet Explorer toolbar. The Explorer Bar opens on the left side of the main Internet Explorer window, where you will see a complete list of all the Web sites you have visited arranged in alphabetic order and grouped by week.

Click a week to expand the entries it contains. If you see a folder icon to the left of the URL, you can click that URL to see a list of all the pages you visited at that Web site. When you click an element from the History folder, the Web site opens in the right side of the main Internet Explorer window.

To close the History folder, click the Close button in the top-right corner, or click the History button on the toolbar a second time.

Subscribing to Sites

In addition to visiting Web sites in the normal way with Internet Explorer, you can subscribe to a Web site. A subscription is a mechanism used by Internet Explorer to check for new or updated content on a Web site without your involvement.

When you subscribe to one of the Web sites on your Favorites menu, Internet Explorer automatically checks the site for new content on a schedule that you specify. You can also choose to be notified when it finds updated content, or you can have Internet Explorer automatically download and store the new material on your hard disk so that you can look at it offline.

To create a new subscription, choose Favorites ➤ Add to Favorites to open the Add Favorite dialog box and then choose one of these options:

 ▶ Yes, but only tell me when this page is updated

 ▶ Yes, notify me of updates and download the page for offline viewing

And to specify the delivery, schedule, and notification options, click the Customize button to open the Web Site Subscription Wizard. You can specify that the Web site is visited daily, weekly, monthly, or when the Update All Subscriptions option is next invoked from the Favorites menu.

To change these subscription settings later, choose Favorites ➤ Manage Subscriptions, right-click the subscription you want to look at or change, and then select Properties.

Tuning In to Channels

A channel is a special Web site designed to deliver content directly to your computer, instead of using Internet Explorer to visit individual Web sites, which is the more traditional method of accessing content.

Choose Favorites ➤ Channels to look at the list of preinstalled channels
on your system. To select a channel in the Explorer Bar, choose View ➤
Explorer Bar ➤ Channels, or simply click the Channels button on the Internet Explorer toolbar.

▲ t i p

The Active Channel Guide is a link to a Microsoft Web site where you will find information on additional channels. There are channels for stock market information,
news services, entertainment information, and financial services, and the list is
growing all the time.

Viewing a Channel

When you view a channel in Windows 98, you open Internet Explorer in a
special full-screen mode that is designed to display as much channel information as possible. The menus and toolbars are hidden, only the Standard
toolbar is available, and you can hide that too if you right-click the toolbar
and choose Auto-Hide from the pop-up menu.

You can view a channel in several ways:

▶ Click the View Channels button on the Quick Launch toolbar.

▶ Click a channel's icon on the Active Desktop Channel bar.

▶ Click the Channels button on the Internet Explorer toolbar.

▶ Choose Favorites ➤ Channels within Internet Explorer.

To close Internet Explorer while in Channel Viewer mode, click the Close
button in the top-right corner of the screen.

Adding a Channel to the Active Desktop

You can also display channels on the Windows 98 Active Desktop. Follow
these steps:

1. Right-click the Active Desktop and then choose Properties from
   the pop-up menu to open the Display Properties dialog box.

2. Select the Web tab and then click New.

3. If you want to visit the Active Desktop Galley Web site, click Yes and choose a channel from there; otherwise, click No.

4. In the New Active Desktop Item dialog box, type the URL or address for the channel in the Location box, or click the Browse button to search for it.

5. When the Subscribe Wizard starts, follow the instructions on the screen. After you download the new content, you will see the new channel displayed on the Active Desktop.

You can also display information from certain channels as a screen saver. Right-click the Active Desktop, choose Properties to open the Display Properties dialog box, and select the Screen Saver tab. In the Screen Saver list, choose Channel Screen Saver, click the Settings button, and configure the screen saver. Not all channels can be used as screen savers.

Searching the Web

At times you'll want to use the Internet to find specific information on a topic, and there are a couple of ways you can use Internet Explorer as an aid in that search. The first way is to perform a straightforward search. Follow these steps:

1. In Internet Explorer, click the Search button on the toolbar.

2. When the Explorer Bar opens on the left side of the main Internet Explorer window, select the search site you want to use.

3. Type the appropriate keywords for your search.

4. Click the button that starts the search. Depending on the search service you use, that button may be labeled something like Start, Search, Submit, or Go.

5. In a few seconds, the search service displays the first page of results. Click the links in that page to explore the Web site for the information you are seeking.

The second kind of search can be even faster and involves the use of the Internet Explorer Address bar. Type **go, find,** or **?** followed by a space and then the word or phrase that you want to find in the Address bar. Internet

Explorer uses a predetermined search mechanism to locate the information you seek. In the list of results, click a link to display the Web page.

▲ t i p
To search the Web from the Start menu, choose Start ➤ Find ➤ On the Internet.

Browsing Offline
You can browse the Web with Internet Explorer without being connected to the Internet. This is because many of the files that you open while browsing the Web are stored in the Temporary Internet Files folder on your hard disk. Choose File ➤ Work Offline, and Internet Explorer will not attempt to connect to the Internet when you select a resource, but will display the copy in the Temporary Internet Files folder instead. To go back to online browsing, choose File ➤ Work Offline a second time.

Speeding Up Internet Explorer
The text component of a Web page downloads quickly, but some of the other common elements, such as graphics, sound files, and animations, can take quite a long time to download.

Of course, there is nothing you can do to change the way a Web site is constructed, but you can stop certain types of files from being downloaded to Internet Explorer. You can essentially tell Internet Explorer to ignore all graphics files or all video clips and just collect the text. Here are the steps:

1.   In Control Panel, click Internet, or choose View ➤ Internet Options within Internet Explorer to open the Internet Options dialog box.

2.   Select the Advanced tab.

3.   Scroll down the list box until you see the Multimedia settings, all of which are selected by default.

4.   Deselect all the items you want to exclude from the Web pages you download to your system.

5.   Click OK to close the Internet Options dialog box.

Remember that these options stay in effect for all subsequent Internet Explorer sessions until you turn them back on.

Installing Applications

You can install applications from floppy disks and CD-ROMs using the Add/Remove Programs applet in the Windows 98 Control Panel. You can also choose Start ➤ Run to invoke an individual Install or Setup program.

Keyboard

 Most of the time you will work with your keyboard without giving it a second thought, but the Keyboard applet in the Control Panel allows you to set several important defaults for keyboard properties, such as the language displayed and at what speed a key must be pressed to be recognized as a repeat key.

To look at or change the keyboard properties, choose Start ➤ Settings ➤ Control Panel ➤ Keyboard to open the Keyboard Properties dialog box. It has two tabs: Speed and Language. The Speed tab contains the following options:

Repeat Delay   Sets the length of time you must hold down a key before the repeat feature kicks in. Drag the slider between Long and Short to get the time you want.

Repeat Rate   Sets the speed at which a character is repeated while a key is held down. Adjust the slider between Slow and Fast to get the repeat rate you want.

Click Here and Hold Down a Key to Test Repeat Rate   Tests the repeat delay and repeat rate speeds that you have chosen.

Cursor Blink Rate   Sets the rate at which the cursor blinks, making the cursor easier to spot in some instances. As you adjust the slider, the sample cursor to the left blinks at the selected rate.

The Language tab contains the following options:

Language and Layout   Displays the language and keyboard layout loaded into memory when the computer is first started. Double-click the highlighted language or layout to open the Language Properties dialog box and select another keyboard layout.

Add   Adds a language and keyboard layout to those loaded into memory when the computer is booted.

Properties   Allows you to change the keyboard layout default. For example, you can choose from at least five keyboard layouts for the United States.

Remove   Deletes the selected language and keyboard layout. It will no longer be loaded into memory when you boot the computer.

Set As Default with More Than One Language Installed   Makes the currently selected language and keyboard layout the default to be used when the computer is started.

Switch Languages   Switches between two or more language and layout settings, as listed above. Click the key combination you want to use to switch the default.

Enable Indicator on Taskbar   Displays a language on the right of the taskbar. Click this indicator to open a dialog box in which you can switch language defaults quickly.

Log Off

 Windows 98 maintains a set of user profiles each containing a different user name, password, Desktop preferences, and Accessibility options. When you log on to Windows 98, your profile ensures that your Desktop settings—including elements such as your own Desktop icons, background image, and other settings—are automatically available to you.

Windows 98 contains an option you can use to log off and log on again as another user quickly and easily. Click the Start button, and then click Log Off *username*. In the Log Off Windows dialog box, click Yes. This closes all your programs, disconnects your system from the network, and prepares the system for use by other users.

Log On

To use Windows 98, you must first log on as a user. Windows 98 maintains a set of user profiles each containing a different user name, password, Desktop preferences, and Accessibility options. This allows several people to use the same computer at different times, and Windows 98 loads a different user profile for each user.

When you log on to Windows 98 and are prompted to enter your user name and password, your profile is loaded to ensure that your Desktop settings—including elements such as your own Desktop icons, background image, and other settings—are automatically available to you.

Unfortunately, you can also press the Esc key to bypass this logon screen and completely circumvent all aspects of Windows logon security. This makes Windows 98 a particularly unsecure system.

If you are connected to a local area network and Windows 98 is configured for that network, you will also be prompted to enter your network password.

✔ **n o t e**

The sequence of dialog boxes that prompt for your user name and password the first time you start Windows 98 will be different from those you see in later sessions. Subsequent sessions will involve fewer steps because you won't be asked to confirm your password.

Maximize/Minimize Buttons

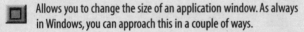 Allows you to change the size of an application window. As always in Windows, you can approach this in a couple of ways.

The Maximize button is in the upper-right corner of an application window, and when you click it, the window expands to full-screen size. Once the window has expanded, the Maximize button changes to the Restore button, which you can then use to shrink the window back to its original starting size.

You can also place the mouse pointer on the window border, and when the two-headed arrow appears, drag the border in the direction in which you want to change its size.

 Use the Minimize button to place an open application on the Taskbar; click the Taskbar icon when you are ready to work with the application again.

Media Player

Allows you to play multimedia files, such as video, animation, and sound clips, depending on the hardware installed on your computer system. You can also change certain settings from the Media Player.

Media Player Dialog Box

Choose Start ➤ Programs ➤ Accessories ➤ Entertainment ➤ Media Player to open the Media Player dialog box. It contains icons that allow you to control the start, stop, and incremental play of the clip.

Play   Starts the clip.

Stop   Halts the playback.

Eject   Ejects the CD-ROM.

Previous Mark   Repositions the clip to the previous marked position.

Rewind   Repositions the clip at the beginning.

Fast Forward   Advances the clip.

Next Mark   Positions the clip at the next marked position.

Start Selection   Marks the beginning of a section of the clip. This is often used along with End Selection to copy a specific part of the clip.

End Selection   Marks the end of a section of the clip.

The slider, located just above the Media Player buttons, indicates your position within the clip or sound file. When a clip is loaded, a scale is displayed beneath the slider. As you drag the slider to the right, the clip advances accordingly. In addition to dragging the slider, you can also click the Scroll Backward or Scroll Forward arrows, located to the right of the slider, to advance the clip in small increments. To move quickly to a general area of the clip, use the slider. You can also use the slider with the Start and End Selection commands to select an area of the clip to copy or to play.

Media Player Menus

The Media Player menus contain options for controlling certain settings for the clip being played, and these options depend on the medium. In addition to the normal menu selections you would expect, you'll find several selections specific to Media Player, as shown in Table 1.

Table 1: Menu Selections Specific to Media Player

Menu	Item	What It Does
Edit	Copy Object	Copies the whole clip to the Clipboard unless you previously chose Selection to isolate a particular portion of the clip.
	Options	Contains settings relevant to the type of file being played.
	Selection	Isolates a portion of the clip.
Device (lists files available for a type of device)	Properties	Allows you to set certain playback options that depend on the device.
	Volume Control	Connects you directly to the Windows Volume Control applet.
Scale*	Time	Sets the scale of the clip to be viewed in time segments.
	Frames	Sets the scale of the clip to be viewed in frames.
	Tracks	Sets the scale of the clip to be viewed in tracks.

*Automatically set according to the device type. You can change this setting for devices that have more than one applicable scale.

Using the Media Player
Media Player contains several command icons and menu items that are available only when a file is open. Follow these steps to get started:

1. Choose Start ➤ Programs ➤ Accessories ➤ Entertainment ➤ Media Player to open the Media Player dialog box.

2. Choose File ➤ Open to open a file of the type you want to play. (The Media folder contains many suitable files.)

m modems

3. Using the toolbar and menus, "play" with the clip.

4. When you are finished, click the Close icon.

t i p

You can also open a file by selecting a device type from the Device menu. Click Device
to display a list of the types of files your computer can play, and then select a file.

Modems

 Allows you to look at or change the settings Windows uses with
your modem. Choose Start ➤ Settings ➤ Control Panel ➤ Modems
to open the Modems Properties dialog box. It contains the General and Diagnostics tabs.

General Tab

Used to remove or edit the properties of your modem. When the tab is first
displayed, it contains the names of the modems currently installed on your
computer.

You have the following options:

Add   Guides you through the installation of your modem. Be sure to
physically connect the modem to your computer and turn it on so that
Windows can sense its presence. You can also specify that you will select
the modem from a list, rather than having Windows search for it.

Remove   Deletes the current modem settings from your computer.

Properties   Displays the Communications Port Properties dialog box,
which has two tabs:

> **General**   Allows you to specify the port used for the modem,
> the speaker volume, and the maximum modem speed to use,
> which is scaled according to your modem's capabilities.

> **Connection**   Sets the number of data bits, the parity, and the
> stop bits settings and specifies certain call preferences, includ-
> ing whether to wait for a dial tone before dialing out and how
> long to wait before canceling an unconnected call. Click the Port
> Settings button to open the Advanced Port Settings dialog box
> where you can set levels for both the receive and the transmit
> buffers; use lower levels if you are having connection problems,

and use higher levels to boost performance. Click the Advanced button to open the Advanced Connection Settings dialog box where you can establish error control, flow control, and other hardware settings.

Dialing Properties   Specifies how your calls are actually made, including the rules for using the area code when dialing, how to dial an outside line, and how to turn off call-waiting services. You can also specify a calling card for use with long-distance calls.

Diagnostics Tab

Identifies which devices are assigned to specific ports, and allows you to look at information on drivers and general items. This tab can help when you want to install a new device but are not sure which ports are in use. It has three buttons:

Driver   Shows the selected device driver file name, its size, and the date the device was installed.

More Info   Shows detailed port information for the selected device and the modem command set.

Help   Gives access to the Windows Help system and the Modem Troubleshooter.

Mouse

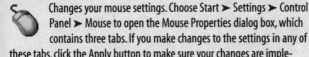 Changes your mouse settings. Choose Start ➤ Settings ➤ Control Panel ➤ Mouse to open the Mouse Properties dialog box, which contains three tabs. If you make changes to the settings in any of these tabs, click the Apply button to make sure your changes are implemented and then click OK.

Buttons Tab

Sets the mouse button configuration and speed with these options:

Button Configuration   Allows you to switch functions from the default right-handed use of the mouse buttons to left-handed. When you select Left-Handed, the left button then performs secondary functions, such as displaying the pop-up menu and performing special drag functions. The right button performs the primary functions of selecting and dragging.   **75**

Double-Click Speed   Allows you to set and then test the speed at which a double-click is recognized. You can increase or decrease the speed with which you must press the mouse button in order for it to be recognized as a double-click.

Pointers Tab

Allows you to change the appearance of the mouse pointer. For example, you can change the pointer used to indicate that Windows is busy from an hour-glass to a symbol or caricature of your choice.

The Scheme box contains the list of pointer schemes available in Windows. By selecting one, you'll see the set of pointers in the scheme displayed in the box below. You can create additional schemes by replacing the individual pointers. Click the Browse button, and select the .ani or .cur files you want. Once you assign the new pointers to the scheme's functions, click Save As to save your new scheme. Clicking Delete removes a scheme, and clicking Use Default restores the original default pointers.

Motion Tab

Controls the pointer speed and the presence of a pointer trail, which makes the mouse pointer much easier to see on LCD screens. If you select a pointer trail, you can also choose whether it is a long or a short trail.

Moving Files and Folders

In Windows, you can move files and folders in three ways:

- ▶ By dragging and dropping
- ▶ By choosing Edit ➤ Cut and Edit ➤ Paste
- ▶ By clicking the right mouse button

When you move a file or folder, you move the original to another location—no duplicate is made.

Using Drag and Drop

To use drag and drop, both the source and the destination folders must be visible, for example, in Explorer or on the Desktop. Hold down the left mouse button and drag the file or folder from one location to the other. When the file or folder reaches the correct destination folder, release the mouse button. The source and destination folders must be on the same drive. If you drag a file or a folder to a different drive, it will be copied rather than moved. If you want to move a file or folder to a different drive, you must drag using the right mouse button.

Using the Edit Menu

The Edit menu in My Computer, Explorer, or any folder window provides a Cut and Paste feature. Here are the steps to follow:

1. Select the file or folder you want to move.

2. Choose Edit ➤ Cut, or click the Cut button on the toolbar.

3. Find the destination file or folder and open it.

4. Choose Edit ➤ Paste, or click the Paste button on the toolbar.

▲ **t i p**

You can select multiple contiguous files or folders to move by holding down Shift and clicking the first and last file or folder. To select noncontiguous files or folders, hold down Ctrl and click the files or folders your want.

Using the Right Mouse Button

Right-clicking a file or folder opens the pop-up menu, which you can use to perform a variety of functions, including moving. Follow these steps:

1. Right-click the file or folder you want to move and select Cut from the pop-up menu.

2. Open the destination folder, right-click, and then select Paste.

▲ **t i p**

If you drag a folder or a file with the right mouse button, a pop-up menu opens when you release the button, allowing you to copy the object, move it, or create a shortcut.

Moving and Arranging Icons

In Windows, you can arrange icons using any of several methods. In Explorer, Control Panel, and many other windows, you can move or arrange icons using the selections in the View menu:

Large Icons   Displays the files and folders as larger-sized icons.

Small Icons   Displays the files and folders as smaller-sized icons.

List   Displays small icons alongside the names of the files and folders.

Details   Displays files and folders in the List style and adds columns for the size of file, date last modified, and type of file. To sort entries within these columns, simply click the column heading. Click once for an ascending sort (A to Z and 0 to 9); click a second time for a descending sort.

Arrange Icons   Opens a submenu you can use to sort the icons by name, type, size, or date. Auto Arrange places the icons on an invisible grid. In My Computer, you can arrange icons by drive letter, type, size, or free space. In Network Neighborhood, you can arrange icons by name or by comment.

Line Up Icons   Rearranges icons into straight vertical and horizontal lines.

▲ t i p

To rearrange icons on the Desktop, simply drag them to their new location. To tidy up the Desktop quickly, right-click an area of free space, and choose Arrange Icons.

By clicking the Views button on the Explorer toolbar, you can cycle the display through the four presentations of Large Icons, Small Icons, List, and Details; each time you click the button, the display changes to the next format.

Multimedia

 Establishes the default settings for multimedia devices connected to your computer; its contents depend on which multimedia devices you have installed.

Choose Start ➤ Settings ➤ Control Panel ➤ Multimedia to open the Multimedia Properties dialog box, containing tabs appropriate to the hardware installed on your computer. You might see the following tabs:

Audio   Sets playback and recording controls.

Video   Specifies the size of the video playback window.

MIDI   Sets Musical Instruments Digital Interface controls and adds new instruments.

CD Music   Sets the drive letter and headphone volume defaults.

Devices   Lists the multimedia hardware connected to your computer and allows you to set or change properties for any of the hardware listed. Select the hardware component you want to configure, and then click Properties to open the related dialog box.

My Computer

 One of the file-management tools available with Windows. You can use My Computer to locate folders, files, and disks or printers on your computer or on mapped drives on other computers connected to the network.

My Computer Folder

Click the My Computer icon on the Desktop to open the My Computer folder, showing an icon for each drive and drive-level folder on your computer. Click an icon to display the contents of one of these folders or drives in a separate window.

Finding a File or Folder with My Computer

When you open My Computer, the My Computer folder displays all the disks and folders on your computer. Follow these steps to find the file or folder you want:

1.   Click the down arrow at the end of the Address toolbar to find the device or folder you want. You will see all the shared disks on your network, important folders such as Control Panel, Printers, and Dial-Up Networking, and other Windows elements, such as

Internet Explorer, Network Neighborhood, Recycle Bin, and My Briefcase. What you see depends, of course, on which Windows components you installed.

2. Click a disk or a folder to see its contents in the window.

3. Once you find the file or folder (which may be several levels down), click it to open it.

✔ n o t e

You can access a remote computer by opening the Dial-Up Networking folder in My Computer. This allows you to establish connections to a remote computer over phone lines using a modem.

My Documents

 A Desktop folder that provides a convenient place to store graphics, documents, or any other files you might want to access quickly. When you save a file in programs such as Paint or Word-Pad, the file is automatically saved in My Documents unless you specify a different destination folder.

To specify a different destination folder, right-click My Documents and select Properties. Type the name of the new folder in the Target field and click OK. Changing to a different folder does not move existing files stored in My Documents.

Naming Disks

You can give a hard or a floppy disk a name that can be a maximum of 11 characters. To name or rename a disk, follow these steps:

1. Open My Computer or Explorer.

2. Right-click the disk you want to name, and select Properties to open the Properties dialog box.

3. Select the General tab, and type the name you want to use for this disk in the Label field. Click OK.

Naming Files and Folders

The first time you save a file using the Save or Save As command, you are asked to provide a name for the file. When you create a new folder, it is always called New Folder until you change the name. Names for files and folders can contain a maximum of 255 characters, including spaces, but cannot contain any of these special characters: / \ ? : * " < > |

Renaming a File or Folder

You can rename both files and folders in Explorer or My Computer. Follow these steps:

1. Open Explorer or My Computer and find the file or folder you want to rename.

2. Click the name once, pause, and then click it again. A box will enclose the name, and the name will be selected. If you move the mouse inside the box, the pointer will become an I-beam.

3. Type the new name or edit the existing name and press Enter.

NetMeeting

A conferencing application that allows people working in different locations to collaborate simultaneously on the same project, sharing Microsoft applications to edit documents. NetMeeting also supports audio and video conferencing over the Internet (as long as you have the appropriate hardware such as a video camera or microphone attached to your computer system), as well as a file-transfer function.

Choose Start ➤ Programs ➤ Internet Explorer ➤ Microsoft NetMeeting to open NetMeeting.

Online Services

Allows you to access several popular online services such as AOL and the Microsoft Network. Before you can use any of these services, you must first register with it. You can do this using the items in the Online Services menu; each item connects you to a specific service. You can also use the Online Services folder on the Desktop.

Before you start, connect your modem to the phone line, and close any other open applications. Each service is a little different in its requirements, but, in general, be ready to supply your name, address, phone number, a credit card number and expiration date, a user name, and a password during the registration process. Simply follow the instructions on the screen to complete your registration.

✔ n o t e

Many of these services use a toll-free 800 number to sign you up as a member. After that, you will use a different telephone number, usually a local number, supplied to you when you register.

Outlook Express

 Windows application used to send and receive e-mail and read and post messages to Internet newsgroups. To start Outlook Express, click the Outlook Express Desktop icon, or choose Start ➤ Programs ➤ Internet Explorer ➤ Outlook Express. You can also click the Launch Outlook Express button on the Quick Launch toolbar, or use the Mail menu from within Internet Explorer.

Outlook Express Window

The main Outlook Express window contains the usual menu bar with a toolbar below and the Outlook Bar arranged down the left side of the window. The central portion of the window contains icons for common activities such as Read Mail, Read News, and Compose a Message.

Outlook Express Toolbars

When you first open Outlook Express, the toolbar contains the following buttons:

 Compose Message Opens the New Message dialog box in which you can create an e-mail message.

 Send and Receive Sends all the e-mail messages in your Outbox and collects all mail waiting for you on the server.

Address Book   Opens Address Book.

 Connect   Connects to the Internet via your ISP.

 Hang Up   Terminates the connection to the Internet.

When you start to work with messages in your Inbox or when you click Compose Message, you will see additional buttons on the toolbar, including:

 Reply to Author   Opens the selected message and lets you compose a reply. The reply is automatically addressed to the original author of the message.

 Reply to All   Opens the selected message so that you can compose a reply. The reply is automatically addressed to everyone who received the original message.

 Forward Message   Opens the selected message so you can forward it to a new recipient.

The Outlook Bar on the left of the Outlook Express window contains these buttons:

 Outlook Express   Returns you to the Outlook Express opening window after you have worked with one of the selections below such as the Inbox or the Outbox.

 Inbox   Contains your most recently received e-mail messages.

 Outbox   Holds the e-mail messages that are waiting to be sent.

 Sent Items   Contains messages that you have sent.

 Deleted Items   Contains messages that you deleted after reading them.

 Drafts   Contains messages in draft form that are not yet ready to be sent.

 News   Contains articles you retrieved from newsgroups.

▲ t i p

The Outlook Bar contains icons that correspond to folders in the Folder List. To see the Folder List, click the Outlook Express icon immediately underneath the toolbar, or choose View ➤ Layout and check the Folder List box. You can also choose View ➤ Layout to place the Outlook Express toolbar at the top, bottom, left, or right of the window; you can even customize the buttons that appear on the toolbar itself.

Outlook Express Menus

All the functions available on the Outlook Express toolbar are also available from the menus, as you would expect, but the menus add a significant number of additional features. Some of the menus, including the File and Edit menus, are dynamic just like the toolbar and add or remove selections depending on where you are in Outlook Express and the nature of the current activity.

Reading Your Mail

Click the Inbox icon on the Outlook Bar to look at your mail; a welcoming message from Microsoft will be waiting for you there. The Preview Pane is divided horizontally; message header information is in the upper pane, and the actual message itself is in the lower pane.

The other major Outlook Express functions all use this dual-pane window; so once you get the hang of it here, it is easy to use the other Outlook Express components.

▲ t i p

You can drag the boundary between these two panes to change the proportions if you wish.

Once you read a message, you can mark it as read or as unread, you can reply to the originator or forward the message to someone else, you can move it to a different folder on the Outlook Bar, or you can delete it. Right-click any message to open the pop-up menu containing selections for all these functions.

You can retrieve your e-mail in several ways:

▶ Click the Send and Receive button on the toolbar in the main Outlook Express window. This also sends any mail waiting in your Outbox.

▶ Choose Tools ➤ Download All.

▶ Choose Tools ➤ Send and Receive. This option works the same
    way as clicking the Send and Receive button on the toolbar.

Creating and Sending a Message

To create a new message, click the Compose Message button on the toolbar
or choose Compose ➤ New Message to open the New Message dialog box
and follow these steps:

1. Enter the e-mail address of the recipient in the To field. If you
    have entered addresses in your Address Book, click the Select
    Recipients from a List icon to open Address Book, and select the
    address from the list.

2. Enter e-mail addresses in the Cc (carbon copy) or Bcc (blind car-
    bon copy) fields if you wish.

3. Enter a subject line for your message; the subject is automatically
    copied into the title bar of this message dialog box.

4. Type the text of your message in the lower part of the dialog box.
    You can create messages in several formats, including Plain Text
    and Rich Text (HTML). The default is Plain Text.

▲ t i p

In the New Message dialog box, use the selections available in the Insert menu
to add other elements to your message, including a signature, business card, horizontal line, picture, or hyperlink.

Once your message is complete, you can send it to the Outbox in several ways:

▶ Click the Send and Receive button on the toolbar in the main Out-
    look Express window. This also retrieves any mail waiting for you
    and places it in your Inbox.

▶ Click the Send icon on the New Message window toolbar.

▶ Choose File ➤ Send Message.

- Choose File ➤ Send Later.

- Choose Tools ➤ Send and Receive.

It makes sense to collect several messages in your Outbox until you are ready to connect to the Internet, rather than sending them one at a time—unless they are urgent, of course. Click the Send and Receive button on the Outlook Express toolbar to connect to the Internet, to send out all the mail from your Outbox, and to pick up all the mail waiting for you and store it in your Inbox.

Attaching a File
To attach a file to an e-mail message, follow these steps:

1. In the New Message window, choose Insert ➤ File Attachment.

2. In the Insert Attachment dialog box, select the file you want to attach, and then click Attach.

3. Your e-mail message now contains an icon indicating that a file is attached, the name of the file, and its size. You can repeat this process to attach additional files as you see fit.

Reading the News
Outlook Express is also a newsreader that you can use to access the thousands of specific-subject newsgroups on the Internet.

✖ w a r n i n g
Anything goes in many of these Internet newsgroups. There is absolutely no censorship, and if you are easily offended (and even if you are not), you might want to stay with the more mainstream groups.

In the same way that you set up an e-mail account with an ISP, you must also set up a newsgroup account, complete with password, before you can use Outlook Express as a newsreader.

You can use Outlook Express to download a complete list of all the newsgroups available to your ISP and then search for newsgroups that might interest you. Once you select a newsgroup, you can read the articles posted to the newsgroup by others, and you can post your own articles using the

Outlook Express e-mail functions; you can even download newsgroup posts and read them later offline to save on connection charges.

Configuring Outlook Express

Configuration options for Outlook Express are quite extensive. You can customize the toolbar and add buttons for the tasks you perform most often, and you can define the rules you want Outlook Express to follow when you are creating, sending, and receiving e-mail. Choose Tools ➤ Options to open the Options dialog box. It has the following tabs:

General Contains general-purpose settings for Outlook Express. The long text descriptions beside each of the checkboxes on this tab make the entries self-explanatory.

Send Specifies the format for sending mail and posting articles to newsgroups, as well as several other mail-related options, such as whether to include the text of the original message in any reply.

Read Specifies options used when displaying articles from newsgroups.

Security Establishes security zones and specifies how Outlook Express manages digital certificates (also known as digital IDs).

Dial Up Specifies the options used when connecting to your ISP by dial-up connection.

Advanced Specifies options of interest only to system administrators.

You can also choose View ➤ Layout to open the Layout Properties dialog box. Click Customize Toolbar to add or remove buttons from the Outlook Express toolbar. To return the toolbar to its original layout, click Customize Toolbar again, and then click Reset followed by Close in the Customize Toolbar dialog box.

Paint

A program with which you can create lines and shapes, with or without color, and place text within graphics. You can also use it to create backgrounds for the Desktop. Choose Start ➤ Programs ➤ Accessories ➤ Paint to open the main Paint window.

Pp paint

Paint Toolbar

Arranged down the left side of the main window, provides tools for drawing and working with color and text. Below the toolbar is an area containing optional choices depending on the type of tool you choose. For example, if you choose the Brush tool, a selection of brush edges is displayed. If you choose Magnifier, a selection of magnifying strengths is displayed. At the bottom of the main window, the Color Palette displays a series of colored squares.

The toolbox contains the following buttons for drawing lines and shapes and for working with color:

 Free-Form Select Selects an irregularly shaped area of the image to move, copy, or edit.

 Select Selects a rectangular shaped area of the image to move, copy, or edit.

 Eraser/Color Eraser Erases an area of the image as you move the eraser tool over it.

 Fill with Color Fills an enclosed area with the currently selected color.

 Pick Color Selects the color of any object you click. It is for use with the tool that you chose immediately before you selected Pick Color.

 Magnifier Enlarges the selected area.

 Pencil Draws a free-hand line one pixel wide.

 Brush Draws lines of different shapes and widths.

 Airbrush Draws using an airbrush of the selected size.

 Text Inserts text onto the drawing. Click Text, click the color you want for the text, and then drag a text box to the location where you want to insert the text. In the font window that appears, click the font, size, and style (Bold, Italic, Underline) you want. Click inside the text box, and begin typing your text.

 Line   Draws a straight line. After dragging the tool to create a line segment, click once to anchor the line before continuing in a different direction, or click twice to end the line.

 Curve   Draws a curved line where one segment ends and another begins. After dragging the tool to create a line segment, click once to anchor the line before continuing. To create a curve, click anywhere on the line and then drag it. Click twice to end the line.

Rectangle   Creates a rectangle. Select the fill style from the toolbar below the main Paint window.

Polygon   Creates a polygon, or figure consisting of straight lines connecting at any angle. After dragging the first line segment, release the mouse, place the pointer where the second line segment is to end, click the mouse button, and repeat until the drawing is complete. Click twice to end the drawing.

 Ellipse   Draws an ellipse. Select the fill style from the Color Palette below the main Paint window.

 Rounded Rectangle   Creates a rectangle with curved corners. Select the fill style from the Color Palette below the main Paint window.

When you create an image in Paint, first select the tool, then select the tool shape, if applicable, and then click the color you want to use from the Color Palette at the bottom of the Paint window. The currently active color is displayed in the top square on the left of the palette. To change the background color, click Pick Color, and then click the color you want. The next image you create will use the new background color.

Paint Menus
Contain many of the standard Windows options. Table 2 shows the menus and their unique options.

Table 2: The Unique Options in the Paint Menus

Menu	Item	Submenu	What It Does
File	Set As Wallpaper (Tiled)		Places the Paint object (when saved) as the background wallpaper, with the design repeated in a tiled design.
	Set As Wallpaper (Centered)		Places the Paint object (when saved) as the background wallpaper, with the design centered.
View	Zoom		Displays a submenu of options for viewing objects.
		Normal Size	Displays an image.
		Large Size	Enlarges an object.
		Custom	Sets specific zoom percentages.
		Show Grid	Displays a grid against the object.
		Show Thumbnail	Displays a thumbnail of the selected part of an object.
	View Bitmap		Displays an image in full-screen view. Pressing any key returns you to the Paint window.
Image	Flip/Rotate		Flips the image horizontally or vertically, and rotates the image 90, 180, or 270 degrees.
	Stretch/Skew		Stretches or skews the object in a horizontal or vertical direction by precise percentages or degrees.
	Invert Colors		Reverses colors or changes them to their complement.
	Attributes		Changes the width and height of the object. You can specify its measurement in inches, centimeters, or pixels, and you can specify colors or black and white.

Table 2 (continued): The Unique Options in the Paint Menus

Menu	Item	Submenu	What It Does
Image	Clear Image		Removes the image from the screen. If you have not saved it, it is lost.
	Draw Opaque		Switches between opaque and transparent drawing. An opaque drawing covers the existing picture; a transparent object allows the underlying picture to show through.
Colors	Edit Colors		Defines custom colors.

Passwords

Allows you to specify a logon password. Windows maintains a set of user profiles, each containing a different user name, password, Desktop preferences, and Accessibility options. When you log on to Windows, your profile ensures that your Desktop settings, including elements such as your own Desktop icons, background image, and other settings, are automatically available to you.

Enabling User Profiles

To enable user profiles, follow these steps:

1. Choose Start ➤ Settings ➤ Control Panel ➤ Passwords to open the Passwords Properties dialog box.

2. Select *Users can customize their preferences and Desktop settings.*

3. In the User Profile Settings box; you can select one option or both:

   ▶ Include Desktop icons and Network Neighborhood content in user settings.

   ▶ Include Start menu and Program groups in user settings.

4. You'll have to use Shut Down to restart your computer for these changes to be applied.

Specifying a Password

When you start Windows 98 for the first time, you are prompted to enter a user name and password and then to confirm that password. If you are connected to a network, you may also be asked to enter a network password. On all subsequent startups, this series of dialog boxes will be slightly different. You will only be asked to enter the password; you will not have to confirm it.

Changing a Password

To change a password, follow these steps:

✔ n o t e

You must know the current password in order to change it.

1. Choose Start ➤ Settings ➤ Control Panel ➤ Passwords to open the Passwords Properties dialog box.

2. Select the Change Passwords tab, and then click the Change Windows Password button to open the Change Windows Password dialog box.

3. Type the old password (asterisks will appear as you type), and enter the new password; you will have to retype the new password to confirm it. Click OK to close the Change Windows Password dialog box.

4. Click OK to close the Passwords Properties dialog box and finalize your new password.

▲ t i p

Next time you log on to Windows, remember to use your new password.

In addition to your logon password, you can establish a password for the following resources:

Dial-Up Connections To change passwords, click My Computer, click the Dial-Up Networking icon, and choose Connections ➤ Dial-Up Server. Click Allow Caller Access to enable the Change Password button. If the Dial-Up Server selection is not available in your Connections

menu, it was not installed along with the other Windows 98 components. Use the Add/Remove Programs applet in Control Panel to complete your installation. Under the Communications heading, be sure
that both Dial-Up Networking and Dial-Up Server are selected for
installation; you need them both to set up a Dial-Up Networking server.

Disks   To set and change passwords, right-click the disk in the
Explorer window and select Sharing from the pop-up menu.

Folders   To change the password or sharing status, open Explorer
or My Computer, select the folder, choose File ➤ Properties, and then
click the Sharing tab.

Printers   To change the password or sharing status, open the Printers folder from Explorer, My Computer, or Control Panel. Right-click the
printer and select Sharing from the pop-up menu. You can also select
the printer, choose File ➤ Properties, and then click the Sharing tab.

Network Administration   Set password access to shared devices
from the Access Control tab in the Network applet in the Control Panel.

Screen Savers   You can use a password to protect others from gain-
ing access to your files when a screen saver is active. To change a password, choose Start ➤ Settings ➤ Control Panel ➤ Display to open the
Display Properties dialog box. Select the Screen Saver tab and click Password Protected, and then click the Change button.

Shared Resources   To change the password or sharing status, open
Explorer or My Computer, select the resource, choose File ➤ Properties
to open the Properties dialog box, and select the Sharing tab. If the
resource is shared, you can change the password. You can also change
the sharing status from the Access Control tab in the Network applet
in the Control Panel.

Click the Change Other Passwords button in the Passwords Properties dialog box to work with these other passwords.

Allowing Remote Administration
You can specify whether a system administrator can create shared folders
and shared printers on your computer, and you can see the user names of
anyone who connects to them by using the options on the Remote Administration tab in the Passwords Properties dialog box.

Paste Command

Copies the contents of the Clipboard into the current document. It is available from the Edit menu and some pop-up menus that are displayed when you right-click a file or a folder.

Path

Defines the information needed to locate a specific file and includes disk drive, folder, subfolder, and file name. For example, the path for the FreeCell game might be C:\Windows\Freecell.exe; C: is the disk drive, \Windows is the folder, and \Freecell.exe is the file name. The backslash (\) separates the different parts of the address.

If the name of a file is more than eight characters or includes blanks or spaces, enclose the full path in quotation marks, such as "C:\FinanceTechnology StocksQuotes.xls".

To specify a path to a folder or a file on the disk drive of another computer that is not mapped to a drive name on your computer, precede the computer name with two backslashes, such as \\Marty\Doc\Budget.doc. Marty is the name of the computer.

To specify a path to a file or folder on another computer that *is* mapped to a drive name on your own computer, type the path as you would for your own disk drive.

Plug and Play

A Windows feature that automatically detects hardware installed in your computer system. Today, most hardware is specifically designed with Plug and Play in mind. You just install the hardware, and Windows takes care of the details, loading the appropriate device drivers and other related software automatically.

Plug and Play adapters contain configuration information stored in permanent memory on the board, including vendor information, serial number, and other configuration data. The Plug and Play hardware allows each adapter to be isolated, one at a time, until Windows identifies all the cards installed in your computer. Once this task is complete, Windows can load and configure the appropriate device drivers. After installing a new Plug and Play adapter in your computer system, Windows will often ask you to restart the system. This is so the new device drivers can be loaded into the correct part of system memory.

Printers

 Manages all functions related to printers and printing. From here you can add a new printer, check on a job in the print queue, change the active printer, or modify a printer's properties.

Printers Folder

To access the Printers folder, choose Start ➤ Settings ➤ Printers. You can also open the Printers applet in the Control Panel or access Printers from My Computer. The Printers folder lists all the printers connected to your computer or available to you on the network. Click the Add Printer icon to start the Add Printer Wizard, which guides you through the process of adding a new printer to your system.

Printing a Document

Unless you specify otherwise, Windows applications pass your documents to the underlying operating system for printing. If you don't specify a printer, Windows automatically sends your document to the default printer. In the Printers folder, the default printer is indicated by a small check inside a darkened circle just above the printer icon.

▲ t i p

When you print a document in Windows, the document is first sent to a temporary disk file rather than directly to the printer. Windows then spools the file to the specified printer. Because Windows is in overall charge of this operation, different print jobs can be queued up, rearranged, deleted, and so on.

You can print a document in three ways:

- ▶ Within your application, choose File ➤ Print, and fill in whatever information you are asked to provide. Some applications have elaborate dialog boxes for choosing a printer, scaling options, or other graphical options, and others simply ask for basic information such as the name of the printer to use, the number of copies you want, and the page range you want to print.

▶   If you arrange your Desktop so that you can see both the document you want to print and the printer icon, you can then simply drag the file to the printer. The original copy of your document is not moved from its folder; it is simply passed to the Windows print spooler for printing.

▶   Right-click a document and note whether the menu contains a Print selection. If it does, you can use the command to print the file; if there is no such option, press Esc.

Print Queue

If you print a large number of files at the same time or if you allow printer sharing by other network users, you may have to check on the status of a print job.

Click the appropriate printer icon in the Printers folder to open the printer queue dialog box, which lists the name of the document being printed or waiting to be printed, the status of the document, the owner of the document, its progress, and when it entered the print queue. The status bar at the bottom of the dialog box displays the number of jobs in the queue.

▲ t i p

The printer queue dialog box is also displayed when you click the printer icon on the Taskbar when a print job is initiated.

The Printer menu contains these specialized options:

Pause Printing   Temporarily interrupts the print job.

Set As Default   Specifies this printer as the default printer.

Purge Print Documents   Deletes all print jobs from the print queue.

Properties   Displays the Properties dialog box for the specified printer.

The Document menu contains the options for starting and stopping printing:

Pause Printing   Temporarily interrupts the print job.

Cancel Printing   Removes a document from the print queue.

✔ **n o t e**

To change the order of documents in a print queue, click the document and drag it to the desired position in the list. You cannot change the order of documents in a network printer queue.

Interrupting Printing

Occasionally, you may need to interrupt a print job. You can do so in three ways:

▶   Click the printer icon on the Taskbar to open the Printer Queue dialog box. Choose Document ➤ Pause Printing or Document ➤ Cancel Printing.

▶   Choose Start ➤ Settings ➤ Printers. Click the printer icon you want to interrupt to display the printer queue dialog box. Choose Document ➤ Pause Printing or Document ➤ Cancel Printing.

▶   Using either the printer icon or the Printers folder, go to the printer queue dialog box, right-click the document you want to interrupt, and select Pause Printing or Cancel Printing.

To continue printing the document, repeat the process described above, only this time remove the checkmark next to Pause Printing.

Printing to a Disk File

Most Print dialog boxes contain an option you can check to print your document to a file rather than to a printer. The file created this way is not a simple copy of your document, but is fully formatted with the codes that control your printer, including font information, page breaks, and even bold and underline attributes.

Once your application creates the file, you can send it to a co-worker as an e-mail attachment or copy it to a floppy. The file can then be printed on any compatible printer.

Printer Properties

Every printer has a collection of associated settings you can look at or change with the Properties dialog box. Because of the huge number of printers of many types now supported by Windows, each with its own individual features, generalizing about what you might see in the Properties dialog box for your printer is difficult.

▲ t i p

To see a quick explanation of what each option in a dialog box does, click the Help question mark icon and then click the option. A small text box explains the option and how to use it.

Choose File ➤ Properties or right-click a printer icon and choose Properties to display that printer's Properties dialog box. You can also press Alt+Enter to open the Properties dialog box. The number of tabs in this dialog box and the options they contain depend on the specific printer attached to your system. Here are some common tabs and options:

General Contains options that allow you to enter comments, specify a separator page to be used between print jobs, and print a test page.

Details Contains options to establish and manage printer ports and drivers. You can also set timeout limits for how long Windows is to wait for a printer to be online, before Windows displays an error message. From this tab, you can also set options for the print spooler.

Sharing Allows you to indicate whether a printer is to be shared and to specify the shared name and password.

Paper Contains settings relating to the size and orientation of the paper. It may contain layout options, page source, and the default number of copies.

Graphics Allows you to specify graphics quality. Settings include graphic image resolution, dithering (blending of colors into patterns) or halftoning, and intensity of image (how light or dark it is).

Fonts Manages fonts, including identifying the font cartridge you want to use, specifying how TrueType fonts are printed, and installing additional fonts.

Device Options   Contains options such as the amount of printer memory available, and lets you adjust printer memory tracking.

Depending on the type of printer, you might also see a PostScript tab or a Color Management tab.

Adding a New Printer

 Click the Add Printer icon in the Printers folder to start the Add Printer Wizard, which guides you through installing a new printer on your system. Here are the steps:

1.   When the Wizard opens, click Next.

2.   Choose whether the printer is a local printer attached to your computer or a network printer connected to another computer. Click Next.

3.   If the printer is a Network printer, fill in the Network path or queue name. Click the Browse button to search for the printer if you are not sure of the path. If you will be using any MS-DOS programs, click Yes for *Do you print from MS-DOS based programs*. If you clicked Yes, you may have to identify a printer port for MS-DOS printing. Click Next and skip to Step 5. If the printer is connected to your own computer, select the name of the maker from the Manufacturers list and the model from the Printers list. If you are manually installing a printer that is not listed, click Have Disk and follow the instructions. After selecting the manufacturer and model, click Next.

4.   Click the port you want to use with the printer, normally LPT1. Click Configure Port to verify that the settings are appropriate and then click Next.

5.   Enter a name for the printer (choose one that you are sure to remember), and then select whether you want to set this printer as your default printer. Click Next.

6.   To print a test page, turn on the printer, load paper if necessary, and click Yes. Otherwise click No, and then click Finish. The printer icon will be added to the Printers folder.

Sharing a Printer

Before other network users can send documents to a printer attached to your system, you must first share the printer. Right-click the printer icon and choose Sharing, or select the printer and choose File ➤ Sharing to open the Properties dialog box at the Sharing tab.

Click Shared As to automatically generate a share name based on the printer name. You can keep this name or change it. Add a comment to indicate where the printer is located so that other network users know where to go to collect their printouts, and add a password if you want to restrict the use of the printer to only those people who know the password. Click OK. If you entered a password, you will be asked to confirm it by entering it a second time. Click OK, and your printer is ready for shared use.

To unshare your printer, open the Properties dialog box, choose the Sharing tab, and click Not Shared.

Programs

Lists the programs available in Windows, either as stand-alone applications or as collections of applications located in submenus or program groups. Any selection that has an arrow pointer to the right of the name is not a single program but a program group. Choosing one of these groups opens another menu listing the items in the group.

Follow these steps to start a program from the Programs menu:

1. Choose Start ➤ Programs to display the current list of program groups.

2. Select a program group to display a list of the programs it contains.

3. Click an application name to start it.

Adding a New Submenu to the Programs Menu

Most Windows programs are added to the Programs menu automatically as they are installed—you are generally asked to verify in which folder or program group any new program should be placed—and the Setup program takes care of the rest. However, you can create a new submenu manually if you wish. Follow these steps:

1. Right-click the Start button and choose Open to open the Start Menu folder.

2. Select the Programs folder, and then choose File ➤ New ➤ Folder. This creates an empty folder in the Program group with the name New Folder.

3. Enter the name you want to use for the submenu as the name of this new folder, press Enter, and then open the folder you just created.

4. Choose File ➤ New ➤ Shortcut to start the Create Shortcut Wizard, which guides you through the process of adding applications to your new folder.

5. Enter the path and file name for the application in the Command Line box, or click the Browse button to locate the file.

6. Type a shortcut name for the program and click Finish.

The next time you open the Programs menu, you will see the entry you just created, and when you select that entry, you will see the list of items that it contains.

Properties

Characteristics of something in Windows—a computer, a peripheral such as a printer or modem, a file, or a folder—are displayed in the Properties dialog box. The properties for any item depend on what it is. To open any Properties dialog box, follow these steps:

1. Select the item in the Explorer.

2. Choose File ➤ Properties.

You can also open the Properties dialog box by right-clicking an object and then selecting Properties from the pop-up menu.

Recycle Bin

 A folder that stores deleted files until they are finally removed from your hard disk. The Recycle Bin is represented on the Desktop by a wastebasket icon. Files are copied to the Recycle Bin both directly and indirectly; you can simply drag a file there, or you can send a file to the Recycle Bin by choosing Delete from a pop-up menu. When you empty the Recycle Bin, the files it contains are permanently removed from your hard disk; once you empty the bin, anything it contained is gone for good.

▲ t i p

If the Recycle Bin contains deleted files, you will see paper protruding from the top of the wastebasket icon.

Recycle Bin Folder

Click the Recycle Bin icon to open the Recycle Bin folder, listing all the files it contains. Choose View ➤ Details to display the original location of the files, the date deleted, the type of file, and its size.

The Recycle Bin menus contain standard Windows options, with the following exceptions in the File menu:

Restore Becomes available when a file is selected, and moves it back to its original directory or folder.

Empty Recycle Bin Deletes files from the Recycle Bin folder and from your hard disk.

Emptying the Recycle Bin

The disk space dedicated to the Recycle Bin is a constant size. Periodically you'll want to empty the Recycle Bin. Follow these steps:

1. Click the Recycle Bin icon on the Desktop to open the Recycle Bin folder.

2. To empty the whole bin, choose File ➤ Empty Recycle Bin. To remove selected files, hold down Ctrl and click the files you want to remove. Then press the Delete key or choose File ➤ Delete.

3. Click Yes to verify that you want to delete the files.

▲ t i p

You can also empty the Recycle Bin by right-clicking the icon and choosing Empty Recycle Bin.

Changing the Size of the Recycle Bin

The initial size of the Recycle Bin is set at 10 percent of the total disk space, but you can change that in the Properties dialog box. If you have more than one hard disk, each hard disk contains its own Recycle Bin. You can allocate the same amount of space for the Recycle Bin on all your disks, or you can configure each hard disk individually. Follow these steps to change the configuration and size:

1. Right-click the Recycle Bin icon and select Properties to open the Recycle Bin Properties dialog box.

3. To use the same amount of hard disk space for the Recycle Bin on all your hard disks, select *Use one setting for all drives* and then drag the slider to the percentage disk space you want to allocate for the Recycle Bin.

4. To specify different sizes for each of the disks on your system, select *Configure drives independently*. Then click the tab for each disk, and drag the slider to the percentage you want to allocate to the Recycle Bin on that disk.

5. Click OK.

Recovering Files from the Recycle Bin

To recover files from the Recycle Bin and move them back to their original folders, follow these steps:

1. Click the Recycle Bin icon.

2. Select the files you want to restore, holding down Ctrl to select multiple files.

3. Choose File ➤ Restore. If you delete a folder and the files it contains, only the files appear in the Recycle Bin. If you restore a file that was originally located in that deleted folder, Windows first re-creates the folder and then restores the file into it.

You can also simply drag a file out of the Recycle Bin or undo the delete operation by choosing Edit ➤ Undo Delete in any folder or Explorer window.

✖ w a r n i n g

If you delete more files than can be held in the disk space allocated for the Recycle Bin, your earliest deleted files will disappear without warning.

Bypassing the Recycle Bin

If hard-disk space is at a premium and you decide to conserve as much space as possible for applications, you can configure Windows to delete files immediately and not copy them into the Recycle Bin. Open the Recycle Bin Properties dialog box, and select the Global tab. Select *Do not move files to the Recycle Bin. Remove files immediately on delete.*

Regional Settings

Sets the systemwide defaults for country (and therefore language), number, currency, time, and date formatting. If you are using English in the United States, you will probably never need Regional Settings; if you want to use a different language, this is the place to start. Choose Start ➤ Settings ➤ Control Panel ➤ Regional Settings to open the Regional Settings Properties dialog box.

Regional Tab

On the Regional Settings tab, click the down arrow and select a language and a country.

▲ t i p

In the Number, Currency, and Time tabs, you will see Appearance Samples boxes. If you change a setting and then click Apply, these samples reflect your new setting. This gives you a chance to review the setting before you make the change permanent.

Number Tab

Sets the defaults for how positive and negative numbers are displayed, the number of decimal places, the separator between groups of numbers, and so on. This tab contains the following options:

Decimal Symbol   Establishes which symbol will be used as a decimal point. The default in the United States is a period.

No. of Digits after Decimal   Specifies how many numbers will be placed to the right of the decimal point. The default is 2.

Digit Grouping Symbol   Determines the symbol that will group digits into a larger number, such as the comma in 999,999. The default is a comma.

No. of Digits in Group   Specifies how many numbers will be grouped together into larger numbers. The default is 3, as in 9,999,999.

Negative Sign Symbol   Establishes which symbol is used to show a negative number. The default is a minus sign.

Negative Number Format   Establishes how a negative number will be displayed. The default is to display the negative sign in front of the number, such as −24.5.

Display Leading Zeroes   Determines whether a zero is shown in front of a decimal number. The default is yes, as in 0.952.

Measurement System   Determines whether the system of measurement will be U.S. or metric.

List Separator   Specifies which symbol will separate items in a list or series. The default is a comma.

If you make any changes in this tab, click Apply and then OK.

Currency Tab

Determines the format for displaying currency. For example, you might want to vary the number of decimal points or the presentation of negative numbers. This tab contains the following options:

Currency Symbol   Displays the symbol of the currency, such as the dollar sign.

Position of Currency Symbol   Shows where the currency symbol is displayed in the number—usually in front of a number.

Negative Number Format   Specifies how negative numbers are displayed.

Decimal Symbol   Determines which symbol separates the whole from the fractional parts of a number, such as a period or a comma.

No. of Digits after Decimal Specifies how many digits are shown by default after the decimal—usually two.

Digit Grouping Symbol Shows which symbol—usually a comma—separates the number groups, such as thousands, millions, and so on.

Number of Digits in Group Specifies how many digits determine a number group, such as 3 for thousands, millions, and so on.

Click Apply and then OK to put any changes you make into effect.

Time Tab

Establishes the default formatting for the time. The Time tab has the following options:

Time Style Determines how the time will be formatted.

Time Separator Determines which symbol separates the hours from the minutes and seconds; the default is a colon.

AM Symbol Specifies the default for the morning symbol.

PM symbol Specifies the default for the afternoon symbol.

Click Apply and then OK to activate any changes you make.

Date Tab

Establishes the default formatting for the date. The Date tab has the following options:

Calendar Type Displays the types of calendars that you can choose from. Think carefully before changing to a different calendar type, as any change will affect the naming and calculation of days, months, and years. You cannot change the calendar from the Gregorian Calendar setting unless you first alter the country and language settings in the Regional Settings tab.

Short Date Style Lists the formats available for displaying the date.

Date Separator Lists the symbols that can be used to separate the month, day, and year.

Long Date Style   Lists the formats available for displaying a formal date notation.

Click Apply and then OK to activate any changes you make.

Restore

Restores an archive copy of one or more files and folders to your hard disk after a disk or controller failure or some other unforeseen event. To start the Windows 98 backup and restore program, choose Start ➤ Programs ➤ Accessories ➤ System Tools ➤ Backup. The first time you start the program, a dialog box welcomes you to Microsoft Backup and leads directly into the Restore Wizard.

Using the Restore Wizard

Using the Restore Wizard is a quick and easy way to learn about restoring backups; it gets you going quickly with the minimum of technical knowledge. Check Restore Backed up Files, and then click OK in this opening dialog box to start the Wizard. If you would rather not use the Wizard, click Close; you can always restart it from the toolbar inside the Backup program if you change your mind.

The Wizard walks you through the following sequence of dialog boxes. Click the Next button when you have made your choice to advance to the next dialog box; click Back to retrace your steps, and click Cancel if you change your mind about using the Wizard.

Restore From   Specify the type and location of the backup you want to restore.

Select Backup Sets   Select a backup set for the restore.

What to Restore   You can restore all files and folders in the backup set, or you can restore selected files and folders.

Where to Restore   Specify the target of the restore; most of the time selecting Original Location to put the file back where it came from makes the most sense.

How to Restore   Specify whether existing files on your hard disk should be overwritten during the restore.

Click the Start button to begin the restore; a small progress indicator tracks the restore as it proceeds.

Using the Restore Tab

Using the Restore tab in the Backup program involves essentially the same tasks that the Restore Wizard does for you—selecting the files, deciding where to put them, and specifying how the restore should actually be made.

✔ note

A checkmark in a gray checkbox means that only some of the files in a folder have been selected. A checkmark in a white box means that all files in a folder have been selected.

Run

 Starts a program or opens a folder when you type its path and name. You often use Run with a Setup program or installation programs or to run a program such as Scanreg that does not have a Windows shortcut. Follow these steps:

1. Choose Start ➤ Run to open the Run dialog box.

2. If you have run this program recently, you may find its name already entered in the Open list box. Click the down arrow, select it by name, and then click OK.

3. If you have not run this program recently or if the Open box is blank, type the full path and program name, such as **C:\Folder\Program**.

4. If you are not sure of the path or program name, click Browse to find and select the program. Then click OK to load and run the program.

ScanDisk

Checks a disk for certain common errors. Once ScanDisk detects these errors, it can fix them and recover any data in corrupted areas. Windows 98 runs ScanDisk automatically if the operating system is shut down improperly, as might happen during a power outage.

Choose Start ➤ Programs ➤ Accessories ➤ System Tools ➤ ScanDisk to open the ScanDisk dialog box. First, select the drive you want to check for errors, and then select the type of test you want to run:

Standard   Tests the selected disk for simple file and folder errors.

Thorough   Runs the standard tests and also scans the disk surface for errors.

If you opt for the Thorough test, you can click the Options button to specify which areas of the disk you want to scan and how they should be tested:

System and Data Areas   Checks the entire disk for errors. This is the most commonly used option.

System Area Only   Checks that portion of the disk occupied by the Windows system files. Much of the information stored in this part of the disk is location-specific and cannot be moved to another area of the disk. Thus, ScanDisk cannot repair any problems in the system area.

Data Area Only   Checks that portion of the disk occupied by your applications and the data files they create. In many cases, ScanDisk can repair errors in this part of the disk and can relocate any data recovered to a known safe part of the disk. The damaged area is then marked so that it will not be used in the future. If the problem is not found early enough, however, data in the damaged area may actually be unreadable. In this case, ScanDisk marks the area of the hard disk as bad.

Do Not Perform Write-Testing   Restricts ScanDisk to performing read tests, which may be less rigorous in unearthing errors and damaged data. Clear this box if you want ScanDisk to perform more rigorous write testing.

Do Not Repair Bad Sectors in Hidden and System Files   Prevents ScanDisk from repairing and moving hidden or system files. In certain cases, moving a hidden or system file to a new location may cause an application not to work properly. Some forms of copy protection require that certain files stay in the same location on disk, and some system files are location-specific and cannot be moved to a new location.

Check the Automatically Fix Errors checkbox if you want ScanDisk to attempt to fix any errors found. If you don't check this box, a dialog box opens when

ScanDisk finds an error, and you can choose whether to repair the error, delete the file, or ignore the error and continue the test scan.

▲ t i p

If you suspect that something serious has happened to your hard disk, try running ScanDisk more than once. You may find that ScanDisk can locate and fix additional errors on each subsequent scan.

Click the Advanced button to open the ScanDisk Advanced Options dialog box. Here you specify how any errors found during testing will be handled:

Display Summary   Displays information about the drive being scanned and any errors discovered and repaired once the scan is complete.

Log File   Records the results of a scan in a file named Scandisk.log.

Cross-Linked Files   Deletes, ignores, or copies two or more files pointing to the same data on a disk.

Lost File Fragments   Deletes or converts fragments that cannot be linked to existing files so you can verify that they are no longer useful.

Check Files For   Looks for invalid and duplicate names and invalid dates and times, which can cause a file to be unreadable or improperly displayed in sorted data.

Check Host Drive First   Checks any uncompressed host drives for errors before checking data on compressed drives created with DoubleSpace or DriveSpace. Be sure this box is checked if you routinely use compressed drives; the host drive may be hidden, and most of the errors on a compressed drive are caused by problems with the associated host drive.

Report MS-DOS Mode Name Length Errors   Reports any errors found in file names.

After setting the options you want, click Start to begin scanning the disk. A status bar across the bottom of the ScanDisk dialog box indicates which area of the disk is being tested and shows the progress of the tests.

When ScanDisk is done, it displays a brief summary of any problems found and fixed on your system, as well as a summary of how the space on the disk is divided among hidden and user files, folders, and free space. Click the Close button to close this report. You can then choose another disk to test from those listed in the main ScanDisk dialog box or click the Close button to close ScanDisk.

Screen Saver

Displays an image on the screen after a fixed period of inactivity. The screen saver hides the normal information displayed by the application you are using and replaces it with another image.

You can change or select a screen saver using the Display applet in the Control Panel. You can set the speed, shape, density, and color of the screen saver, and you can set a password to get back to your work and other settings. You can also use certain active channels as screensavers.

Send To

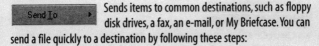 Sends items to common destinations, such as floppy disk drives, a fax, an e-mail, or My Briefcase. You can send a file quickly to a destination by following these steps:

1. Right-click the file or folder to open the pop-up menu.

2. Select Send To.

3. Click the appropriate destination.

Settings

 Choose Start ➤ Settings to access all the Windows 98 configuration tools, including the Control Panel, Printers, Taskbar & Start Menu, Folder Options, and the Active Desktop controls.

Shortcuts

Quick ways to open an application or access a disk, file, folder, printer, or computer without going to its permanent location using the Windows Explorer. Shortcuts are useful for applications that you use frequently; when you access a shortcut, the file, folder, printer, computer, or program is opened for you. You can create a shortcut using the File menu, pop-up menus, or drag-and-copy.

Using Menus

To create a shortcut using menus, follow these steps:

1. Find and select the item for which you want to create a shortcut using My Computer or Explorer. (In Explorer, be sure that the object is displayed in the pane on the right.)

2. Choose File ➤ Create Shortcut. The shortcut is created and appears in the pane on the right.

3. Drag the shortcut where you want it.

Using a Pop-Up Menu

A quicker way to create a shortcut—in My Computer, Explorer, or on the Desktop—is to right-click the item and then choose Create Shortcut from the pop-up menu.

Using Drag and Copy

You can create a shortcut by dragging the item for which you want a short-cut to its destination, such as another folder or the Desktop, while pressing Ctrl+Shift. (Pressing Shift moves a file; Ctrl copies a file; Ctrl+Shift creates a shortcut for it.) You can also drag the item with the right mouse button. When you finish dragging, Windows displays a pop-up menu from which you can choose Create Shortcut.

▲ t i p

To change the properties of a shortcut, such as what sort of window it starts in, right-click the shortcut and choose Properties.

Adding a Submenu to the Programs Menu

You can also add a shortcut to the Programs menu by creating a new sub-menu. Follow these steps:

1. Right-click the Start button, and then choose Open.

2. Select the Programs folder.

3.   Choose File ➤ New ➤ Folder.

4.   Enter the name you want to use for the new submenu.

5.   Press Enter and then open the folder you just created.

6.   Choose File ➤ New ➤ Shortcut.

7.   Follow the directions given by the Create Shortcut Wizard to add new items to the submenu.

✔ n o t e

Deleting a shortcut does not delete the original item; it still remains on the disk. To delete a shortcut, simply drag it to the Recycle Bin.

Shut Down

 The procedure for closing Windows. You must always follow the Shut Down procedure before turning your computer off or restarting your system; if you don't, you run the risk of losing data. Follow these steps to shut down:

1.   When you are ready to turn off your computer, choose Start ➤ Shut Down to open the Shut Down Windows dialog box. It contains the following options:

   Shut Down   Prepares the computer to be turned off.

   Restart   Prepares the computer for shut down and then automatically starts it again.

   Restart in MS-DOS Mode   Closes Windows and restarts the computer in MS-DOS mode.

2.   Select the option you want, and then click OK.

3.   Respond to any other questions that Windows displays.

When Windows 98 has finished saving data to your hard disk, it displays a final message telling you that it is now safe to turn off your computer.

Sounds

 Assigns sounds to certain system events, such as warning dialog boxes, and to more common events such as opening or closing windows or receiving an e-mail message. Choose Start ➤ Settings ➤ Control Panel ➤ Sounds to open the Sounds Properties dialog box. It contains the following options:

Events   Lists the Windows events to which you can assign sounds. If an event has a loudspeaker icon to its left, a sound is assigned to it, which you can change.

Sound Name   Selects the name of the sound that you want to assign to an event. This option becomes available when you click an event.

Browse   Searches through the available sounds. Sounds are usually contained in a .wav file.

Preview   Plays the sound, if you have a sound card and speakers. When a Sound Name is selected, the Preview becomes available.

Details   Displays the selected sound's Properties dialog box containing a copyright statement (if the sound is copyrighted), its time length, data format, creator, and so on.

Schemes   Lists sets of events with particular sounds assigned to the listed events. Windows Default is the name of the default scheme. The set of associated sounds is displayed under Events. You can change the sounds associated with the schemes and then save them under a different name, if you want. Choose None from the Schemes list to silence all these sounds when you use your system in the library.

Follow these steps to assign a sound to an event:

1.   Choose Start ➤ Settings ➤ Control Panel ➤ Sounds to open the Sounds Properties dialog box.

2.   Click an event to which you want to assign a sound or change the default sound.

3. Assign a sound from the selections in the Name drop-down list box. If you don't know the sound you want, click Browse to see a list of available sounds.

4. Click a sound, and then click the Preview arrow to hear it. Continue to select sounds and preview them until you have the sound you want. Click OK twice.

5. Save the set of sounds by clicking Save As and typing a new name. Click OK.

You can always go back to the original Windows sounds by selecting Windows Default from the Schemes list box.

Start

Start The primary way to access files, folders, and programs on your computer. Initially, the Start button is on the bottom left of your screen at the left end of the Taskbar. Click Start to display the Start menu. Some of the options on this menu are standard with Windows 98, but you can add others to give you fast access to your favorite applications.

The Start menu contains the following options:

Shut Down Prepares the computer to be shut down or restarted.

Log Off Logs off the system quickly so that you can log back on with a different user profile or so that another user can log on.

Run Opens the Run dialog box so that you can run a program or open a folder by typing its path and name.

Help Opens the extensive Windows 98 Help System.

Find Searches for a file, folder, device, or computer. You can also search the Internet and look for personal contact information.

Settings Accesses the Control Panel, Printers, Taskbar & Start Menu, Folder Options, and Active Desktop controls so that you can configure the way Windows operates.

Documents Gives you access to the last 15 documents you opened.

Favorites   Gives you access to Channels, Links, and Software Updates.

Programs   Gives you access to the program groups and files on your computer.

Windows Update   Automatically connects to the Microsoft Web site to check for updates to the Windows 98 operating system.

▲ t i p

To add a program or a shortcut to the Start menu, simply drag its icon to the Start button.

Subscriptions
→See Internet Explorer

StartUp

An application that is activated automatically each time you start Windows. If you use certain applications frequently and do not want the bother of starting them manually every time you start Windows, simply put them in your StartUp folder. Follow these steps:

1. Choose Start ➤ Settings ➤ Taskbar & Start Menu to open the Taskbar Properties dialog box.

2. Select the Start Menu Programs tab.

3. Click Add, and type the name of the path to the program you want, or click Browse to find it. Click Next.

4. Find the StartUp folder in the list of Start Menu folders, and select it. Click Next.

5. If you don't like the default, type the shortcut name that you want to appear in the StartUp folder, and click Finish.

6. If you are prompted to choose an icon, click one, and then click Finish.

7. To verify that the program you selected is now in the StartUp menu, choose Start ➤ Programs ➤ StartUp.

The next time you start Windows 98, the program you just added to the StartUp folder will be automatically loaded.

Taskbar

Launches programs and is the primary tool for switching from one application to another. The Taskbar contains several types of icons:

▶   The Start button at the left end of the Taskbar is responsible for launching applications, opening documents, and adjusting settings.

▶   The Quick Launch toolbar contains buttons you can use to do the following:

> ▶   Open Internet Explorer
>
> ▶   Open Outlook Express
>
> ▶   Open TV Viewer
>
> ▶   Bring the Desktop to the front
>
> ▶   View channels

▶   Any shortcut buttons to the right of the Quick Launch toolbar represent the applications currently active in memory or open folders. You can use these icons to switch between the running applications.

▶   The system clock at the right end of the Taskbar displays the current time.

The Taskbar may also show other icons from time to time, indicating that an e-mail message is waiting, that you are printing a document, or the battery condition on a laptop computer.

Switching with the Taskbar

When you open a new application, the Taskbar gets another button, and by clicking that button, you can switch to the new application or folder. For the first few programs, the buttons on the Taskbar are long enough so that you can read the complete names of your applications. As you open more programs and add more buttons to the Taskbar, these buttons have to get smaller and smaller to fit, and so the names are truncated. If you really want to see the complete application names, you can resize the Taskbar and give it an additional line of buttons; simply drag the top edge of the Taskbar upward. The downside of this is that you reduce the effective size of your Desktop.

Switching with Alt+Tab

You can also use the Alt+Tab key combination to switch between running applications. Press and hold down the Alt key and press the Tab key once to open a dialog box that contains an icon for each application running on your system. Each time you press the Tab key, the outline box moves one icon to the right until it wraps all the way round and reappears on the left side of the box. This outline box indicates the application that will run when you release the Alt key.

The name of each application or folder is displayed at the bottom of the box, which is particularly useful when you are switching between folders as they all use the same icon.

Taskbar & Start Menu

The Taskbar is the main way that you switch from one application to another in Windows 98. The default Taskbar contains two types of buttons: the Start button, and any number of shortcut buttons for the applications currently active in memory.

To change how the Taskbar looks and works, choose Start ➤ Settings ➤ Taskbar & Start Menu to open the Taskbar Properties dialog box. You can also choose a toolbar from a set of default toolbars and add it to your Taskbar; you can even create your own custom toolbar.

▲ t i p
You don't have to leave the Windows Taskbar at the bottom of the screen; you can place it along any of the four edges. To move it, simply drag it to its new location.

Modifying the Taskbar Display

The Taskbar is usually at the bottom of the screen and is always displayed on top of other windows so that you can get to it quickly and easily. To change how the Taskbar is displayed, follow these steps:

1. Choose Start ➤ Settings ➤ Taskbar & Start Menu to open the Taskbar Properties dialog box. You can also simply right-click an empty spot on the Taskbar and select Properties from the pop-up menu.

2. Place a checkmark in the checkbox next to the options you want:

    Always on Top   Forces the Taskbar to remain on top of other windows, ensuring that it is always visible to you.

    Auto Hide   Displays the Taskbar as a small thin line on the bottom of the screen. To also display the thin line when a full-screen window is displayed, select both Always on Top and Auto Hide.

    Show Small Icons in Start Menu   Displays a small Start menu with smaller icons.

    Show Clock   Displays the time in the left of the Taskbar. By double-clicking the clock, you can reset the time or date.

3. Click Apply to make the changes final, and then click OK.

▲ t i p

Instead of using Auto Hide, you can shrink the Taskbar by dragging its top edge downward; to redisplay the Taskbar, simply drag its visible edge upward. To redisplay the Taskbar when Auto Hide is selected, place the pointer on the thin line on the bottom of the screen. The Taskbar will automatically reappear.

Adding Toolbars

Windows 98 includes a default set of toolbars that you can add to your Taskbar if you wish:

Address   Allows you to open an Internet address without first opening Internet Explorer.

Links   Contains a set of Internet addresses.

Desktop Adds all your Desktop icons to the Taskbar. Because this toolbar is longer than the screen is wide, you can use the small arrows to see the other icons.

Quick Launch Contains buttons you can use to do the following:

- Open Internet Explorer
- Open Outlook Express
- Open TV Viewer
- Bring the Desktop to the front
- View channels

To add one of these toolbars to your Taskbar, right-click an empty spot on the Taskbar, choose Toolbars from the pop-up menu, and then select the toolbar you want to add to your Taskbar.

▲ t i p

You can also add your own shortcut to the Quick Launch toolbar. Open My Computer or Explorer, select the application you want to add, and drag it to the Quick Launch part of the Windows Taskbar. You will see that program's icon appear next to the other icons on the Quick Launch toolbar. To remove an icon from the Quick Launch toolbar, right-click it and choose Delete.

Creating a Custom Toolbar

If the default toolbars don't meet your needs, you can always create your own. Follow these steps:

1. Right-click an empty part of the Taskbar to open the pop-up menu.

2. Choose Toolbars ➤ New Toolbar to open the New Toolbar dialog box.

3. Select a folder from the list or type an Internet address that you want to appear as a toolbar.

Another way to build a custom toolbar is to create a new folder, add all your favorite shortcuts to it, and then choose Toolbars ➤ New Toolbar to turn it into a toolbar.

This can obviously get out of hand in a hurry, with custom toolbars appearing all over the place, so be careful to create them only as you need them, and then it's probably best if you confine them to the Taskbar.

▲ t i p
To move a toolbar to the Desktop, simply drag it to the new location and then size it as you see fit.

Task Scheduler

A program you can use to run selected applications at specific times—daily, weekly or even monthly—without any input from you or involvement on your part. The Task Scheduler starts running in the background every time you start Windows 98; it just sits there until it is time to run one of your selected tasks, and then it moves into action.

Certain tasks are well-suited to unattended automatic operation, such as making a tape backup or running the hard-disk utilities ScanDisk and Disk Defragmenter. You can run these programs while you work, but often it makes more sense to run them when your system is turned on but not too busy, such as at lunch time, when you are attending a regularly scheduled company meeting, or during the night.

To open the Task Scheduler, you can either double-click the Task Scheduler icon on the Taskbar or open the Scheduled Tasks folder in My Computer. Either way, you will see the main Task Scheduler window. Any currently scheduled tasks are listed in the main window along with information about when they will next run and when they last ran.

Adding a New Scheduled Task
To add a new scheduled task, follow these steps:

1. Open the Scheduled Tasks folder in My Computer or double-click the Task Scheduler icon on the Taskbar to open Task Scheduler.

2.   Click Add Scheduled Task to open the Add Scheduled Task Wizard.

3.   Follow the instructions on the screen.

To modify an existing task, right-click the task, and then choose Properties from the pop-up menu:

Task   Changes the name of the program you want to schedule.

Schedule   Changes when the program is run.

Settings   Customizes the task configuration.

To halt a scheduled task that is currently executing, right-click to open the pop-up menu, and then select End Task; to resume the task, right-click and choose Run. To remove a task, right-click and select Delete from the pop-up menu.

Using the Advanced Menu

The Task Scheduler Advanced menu includes the following options:

Stop Using Task Scheduler   Turns the Task Scheduler application off and halts all scheduled tasks. Task Scheduler will not start automatically the next time you start Windows. This menu selection changes into Start Using Task Scheduler so that you can use it to restart operations.

Pause Task Scheduler   Temporarily stops the Task Scheduler. This menu item changes into Continue Task Scheduler so that you can restart operations. Any tasks that were due to run during the time Task Scheduler was paused will not run until their next scheduled time.

Notify Me of Missed Tasks   Informs you of any scheduled tasks that did not run.

View Log   Opens the Task Scheduler log file in a Notepad window.

Toolbar

→See Taskbar & Start Menu

Undeleting Files

 When you delete a file or a folder, it is stored in the Recycle Bin, but until you actually empty the Recycle Bin, you can still retrieve any files you deleted. To recover a file from the Recycle Bin and return it to its original location, follow these steps:

1. Click the Recycle Bin on the Desktop.

2. Select the file or files you want to restore.

3. Right-click and choose Restore, or choose File ➤ Restore.

If you have chosen to display the contents of the Recycle Bin as a Web page, you can also click Restore All to return multiple files to their original locations.

▲ **t i p**
To select multiple files, hold down Ctrl while you click.

Uninstalling Applications

 The Uninstall program removes all traces that an application was ever installed. It removes all references to the program from the Windows directories and subdirectories and from the Windows Registry.

The Uninstall feature is found in the Add/Remove Program Properties dialog box. Follow these steps to uninstall a program:

1. Choose Start ➤ Settings ➤ Control Panel ➤ Add/Remove Programs to open the Add/Remove Programs Properties dialog box.

2. If necessary, select the Install/Uninstall tab.

3. Select the software you want to remove from the list and click Add/Remove.

User Profiles
➔*See Profiles*

Users

 Windows 98 maintains a set of user profiles each containing a different user name, password, Desktop preferences, and Accessibility options. When you log on to Windows 98, your profile ensures that your Desktop settings—including elements such as your own Desktop icons, background image, and other settings—are automatically available to you.

To set up a new user profile, follow these steps:

1. Choose Start ➤ Settings➤ Control Panel ➤ Users to open the Enable Multi-User Settings dialog box.

2. Click the Next button.

3. In the Add User dialog box, enter your user name and click Next.

4. In the Enter New Password dialog box, type your password. Type it again in the Confirm Password field and click Next.

5. In the Personalized Items Settings dialog box, select the items from the list that you want to personalize, and then choose whether you want to create copies of these items or create new items in order to save hard-disk space. Click the Next button.

6. Click the Finish button to complete the creation of this new user profile and to close the Wizard.

Volume Control

An accessory you can use to control the volume of your sound card and speakers. If you have more than one multimedia capability installed, for example, MIDI or Wave-handling capability, you can control the volume and balance for each device separately. Follow these steps to access the Volume Control:

1. Choose Start ➤ Programs ➤ Accessories ➤ Entertainment ➤ Volume Control to open the Volume Control dialog box. It contains separate features to balance volume for the devices on your computer. Depending on the hardware installed on your computer, the following features may or may not appear:

Volume Control   Controls volume and balance for sounds coming out of your computer. This is the "master" control.

Line-In   Controls the volume and balance for an external device that feeds sound into your computer, such as audio tape or an FM tuner.

Wave Out   Controls the volume and balance for playing .wav files as they come into the computer.

MIDI   Controls the volume and balance for incoming sounds from MIDI files.

Audio-CD   Controls the volume and balance for CD-ROM audio files as they come into the computer.

Microphone   Controls the volume and balance for sound coming in via a microphone.

2. To control the volume of the components, move the vertical slider labeled Volume up or down to increase or decrease volume.

3. To control the balance between two speakers, move the horizontal slider labeled Balance to the left or right to move the emphasis to the left or right speaker.

4. Click Mute All or Mute to silence all components' or one component's contribution to the sound.

Varying the Recording Volume

To vary the volume and balance when you are recording, follow these steps:

1. From the Volume Control dialog box, choose Options ➤ Properties to open the Properties dialog box.

2. Select Recording to display a list of devices that apply to the recording task.

3. If it is not already checked, click the checkbox to select the device you want.

4. Click OK to open the Recording Control dialog box for the selected device.

5. Move the Balance and Volume sliders to adjust the volume and balance of the sound.

Adjusting Playback Sound Quality

The Volume Control dialog box displays all the devices it knows about that relate to playback or the output of sound. If the device you want to adjust is not on the list, follow these steps to select the device:

1. From the Volume Control dialog box, choose Options ➤ Properties to open the Properties dialog box.

2. Select Playback to display a list of applicable devices.

3. If it is not already selected, click the device you want.

4. Click OK to open the Volume Control dialog box, which displays the selected devices.

5. Adjust the Balance and Volume as needed.

▲ t i p

To control the volume and balance for voice command devices, select Other from the Properties dialog box, and then select Voice Commands from the drop-down list box. A list of voice command devices installed on your computer will be displayed in the text box.

What's This

What's This?   Provides context-sensitive help in some dialog boxes. If you right-click an item in a dialog box, a small menu opens containing the single selection What's This. Click What's This to display help text for that specific item.

Other dialog boxes have a Help button in the upper-right corner (look for the button with a question mark on it) next to the Close button. When you click this Help button, the question mark jumps onto the cursor; move the cursor to the entry on the dialog box that you want help with and click again. A small window containing the help text opens; click the mouse to close this window when you are done.

Windows Update

Connects to the Windows Update Web site and keeps your system up-to-date by automatically downloading new device drivers and Windows system updates as they are needed. Choose Start ➤ Windows Update, or choose Start ➤ Settings ➤ Windows Update. Internet Explorer opens and connects to the Web site. The Wizard scans your system looking for items that could be updated. It makes a list of any new device drivers or system patches that you need and then downloads and installs the files for any items you want to update.

You will also find current information on using Windows 98 on the Windows Update Web site as well as a set of answers to frequently asked questions about Windows. Simply follow the instructions on the screen.

Winipcfg

A program you can use to find your IP address when connected to the Internet. To run this program, connect to the Internet using your ISP, and then follow these steps:

1. Choose Start ➤ Run to open the Run dialog box.

2. In the Open text box, type **winipcfg** and then click OK to open the IP Configuration dialog box.

Much of the information listed here is of a highly technical nature and is only of interest to system administrators who will use winipcfg when troubleshooting an Internet connection.

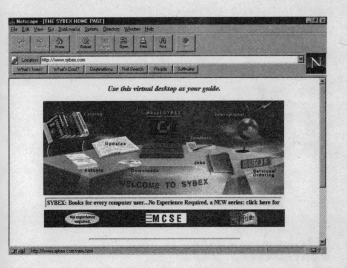

ABCs of Windows 98
by Sharon Crawford
ISBN: 0-7821-1953-0; 384 pages; $19.99

This tutorial helps beginners learn Windows 98 quickly and easily.

Windows 98:
No Experience Required
by Sharon Crawford
ISBN: 0-7821-2128-4; 608 pages; $24.99

This is the most comprehensive beginner/intermediate tutorial on the market. It takes readers beyond where the competitive reference guides leave off.